U.S. House of Representatives
Committee on Oversight and Government Reform
Jason Chaffetz (UT-3), Chairman

FOIA Is Broken: A Report

Staff Report
114th Congress

January 2016

"The Freedom of Information Act should be administered with a clear presumption: In the face of doubt, openness prevails. . . . All agencies should adopt a presumption in favor of disclosure, in order to renew their commitment to the principles embodied in FOIA, and to usher in a new era of open Government. The presumption of disclosure should be applied to all decisions involving FOIA."

--President Barack Obama
January 21, 2009

"Despite prior admonitions from this Court and others, EPA continues to demonstrate a lack of respect for the FOIA process. . . . The Court is left wonder whether EPA has learned from its mistakes or if it will merely continue to address FOIA requests in the clumsy manner that has seemingly become its custom. Given the offensively unapologetic nature of EPA's recent withdrawal notice, the Court is not optimistic that the agency has learned anything."

--Landmark Legal v. EPA, No. 12-1726 (D.D.C.)
March 2, 2015

Executive Summary

Since President Lyndon Johnson signed the Freedom of Information Act (FOIA) in 1966, the FOIA request has been used millions of times for a myriad of reasons. FOIA is one of the central tools to create transparency in the Federal government. FOIA should be a valuable mechanism protecting against an insulated government operating in the dark, giving the American people the access to the government they deserve. As such, FOIA's promise is central to the Committee's mission of increasing transparency throughout the Federal government.

The power of FOIA as a research and transparency tool is fading. Excessive delays and redactions undermine its value. In large part, FOIA's efficacy is limited by the responsiveness of the agency that receives and processes the request. On innumerable occasions, agencies have refused to produce documents or intentionally extended the timeline for document production to stymie a request for information. In many cases, American citizens find themselves frustrated by the total lack of response from the government they are asked to trust.

In light of numerous reports of delays and obstruction related to the FOIA process, the Committee sought feedback directly from FOIA stakeholders, including via an online portal where requesters submitted cases highlighting ineffective or inefficient FOIA processes. The Committee asked for examples of delays, abusive fees, inappropriate redactions, and other tactics frustrating the FOIA process. In a matter of weeks, the Committee received a plethora of responses.

The comments were enlightening. Members of the media described their complete abandonment of the FOIA request as a tool because delays and redactions made the request process wholly useless for reporting to the public. Experienced FOIA users shared "worst of the worst" examples and offered suggestions for reform. First-time or infrequent requesters, however, shared the most disheartening responses. Novice FOIA requesters were unprepared for the delay tactics and other obstacles to obtaining the information they were seeking. One 26 year-old freelance journalist wrote to the Committee about his first experience with FOIA, "I often describe the handling of my FOIA request as the single most disillusioning experience of my life."

On June 2 and 3, 2015, the Committee explored the FOIA experience with two hearings involving more than fifteen witnesses. On the first day, journalists, media organizations, FOIA experts, and transparency advocates testified to the numerous burdens facing FOIA requesters. The next day, select agencies appeared before the Committee to explain barriers to effective and efficient FOIA compliance and what the Committee could do to improve the process.

This report draws on the testimony and comments received by the Committee to illustrate the barriers to access that citizens face with respect to FOIA. The examples call attention to the need for legislative FOIA reform. To that end, while oversight of FOIA and other transparency tools will continue, the Committee will simultaneously identify solutions and pursue needed legislative reform.

Findings

The Executive Branch culture encourages an unlawful presumption in favor of secrecy when responding to Freedom of Information Act requests.

> ➢ "We live in constant fear of upsetting the WH (White House)," said one government employee. (See page three)

> ➢ White House policy requires consultation on FOIA requests that contain "White House equities," which slows the response process and encourages the use of exemptions. (See pages two and three)

The Administration is unaware that FOIA is systemically broken.

> ➢ A Department of Justice report graded agencies on FOIA compliance, giving high marks to some of the worst performing agencies. For example, the Department of State received near top scores in most categories despite an average wait time of three months for simple requests. (See page seven)

Agencies overuse and misapply exemptions, withholding information and records rightfully owed to FOIA requesters.

> ➢ The Federal Communications Commission redacted the Chairman's name and initials in official, work related emails, making it difficult for requesters to determine who at the agency is accountable for any decisions, based on a clearly improper use of the privacy exemption. (See pages 17-19)

> ➢ A requester asked for the curriculum vitae (CV) of advisors to the Food and Drug Administration (FDA). College professor commonly post their entire unredacted CVs online. However, FDA redacted information on curriculum vitae of advisors, claiming the CVs contained confidential business information and privacy information. (See page 20)

FOIA requesters face agency roadblocks and struggle to decipher unclear communications from agency FOIA offices.

> ➢ An individual made a FOIA request of Customs and Border Patrol for documents related to his own communications and travel. Nearly a year later, CBP responded but only after Congress inquired about the status of the request. (See page 37)

While the statute lays out simple requirements to make a FOIA request, every agency has different policies, fee schedules, and levels of complexity to obtain records, creating an unwelcoming environment for the novice requester.

➤ The Department of State denied a request for a contract because State could not reasonably identify the record using the contractor's name. Instead, the Agency suggested the requester could obtain more specific information, such as the contract number, from a database known for having inaccurate data – creating a situation where the requester effectively needed the contract in order to get the contract. (See pages 26-27)

➤ In searching for documents responsive to a request, the General Services Administration (GSA) identified more records than initially anticipated. Despite the requester repeatedly confirming that all of the documents identified were of interest and he would be willing to pay for the documents, GSA refused to provide the records, stating "We don't want to charge you for information that is not responsive to your request." (See pages 27-29)

Agencies create and follow FOIA policies that appear to be designed to deter requesters from pursuing requests and create barriers to accessing records.

➤ Waiting for responses can take so long that at one organization an individual made a request, left the organization to pursue a graduate degree, worked for years with another organization, and return to the original organization before receiving an initial response. (See page 31)

➤ Excessive fees are a persistent problem. For example, the Drug Enforcement Agency charged a FOIA requester nearly $1.5 million for one request. (See page 32)

Many agency FOIA offices have abandoned the statutory requirement to make a determination within 20 working days, or 30 working days in unusual circumstances.

➤ Syracuse University conducted a study on agency responses to FOIA requests. After four months, two thirds of the agencies had failed to produce documents. Most of the remaining agencies were severely delinquent, including the Department of Justice Office of Information Policy, which oversees FOIA processes for the rest of the federal government. (See page 35-36)

➤ In July 2013, a Ph.D. candidate requested records from the State Department necessary to complete his dissertation. In October 2015, he received a fourth extension notice with a completion date of April 2016. (See page 36)

FOIA requesters have good reason to mistrust even fair and earnest attempts by agencies to fulfill requests.

➤ In the words of one requester, "[s]omething is desperately wrong with the process. It is either totally broken or requests are intentionally being ignored." (See page 38-39)

Table of Contents

Introduction

On March 2, 2015, the United States District Court for the District of Columbia chastised the Environmental Protection Agency (EPA) for its "continued disregard for its FOIA obligations."[1] The Court described a culture of unrepentant noncompliance with Federal law and disrespect for the FOIA process, which resulted in the deletion of potentially responsive records and inexplicable delays.[2] Even while engaged in the lawsuit, EPA continued a pattern of unresponsiveness, incomplete document searches, and deletions.[3]

In July of 2015, another Federal District Court Judge admonished the Department of State (State) for excessive delays responding to FOIA requests from the Associated Press (AP) for documents about former Secretary of State Hillary Clinton's schedules and her top staffers.[4] Discussing State's inability to produce a set of 60 emails, the judge stated, "[n]ow, any person should be able to review that in one day—one day. Even the least ambitious bureaucrat could do this."[5] The Judge also expressed concerns about the delays in collecting the records, stating, "[i]t appears they didn't get anything done for two years."

The Courts' comments in both of these cases reflect sentiments applicable across the Executive Branch. Requesters are required to interact with federal agencies that "demonstrate[] apathy and carelessness" toward FOIA requests "to an extent that understandably raises public suspicion."[6] Delays, redactions, and demands for unreasonable specificity from requesters who quite obviously do not have first-hand knowledge of the documents create the impression that the agencies have an "utter indifference to . . . FOIA obligations."[7]

Instead of taking action to fix these problems, the Administration seems willfully blind to the condition of the FOIA process. In a 2015 annual report, the Department of Justice (DOJ) rated agencies' FOIA programs on a number of self-determined factors, resulting in top scores for many of the worst performing agencies.[8] DOJ touts that 91 percent of requests reviewed for disclosure were released in whole or part. While true, the reality is that more than 70 percent of requests were withheld in whole or in part, or not reviewed for disclosure at all. Only 28 percent of requesters received all responsive records and information requested.

---

[1] Landmark Legal Found. v. EPA, 2015 U.S. Dist. LEXIS 24620 (D.D.C. Mar. 2, 2015).
[2] *Id.*
[3] *Id.*
[4] Rachel Bade, *Judge Explodes Over Hillary Email Delays,* POLITICO, July 29, 2015, http://www.politico.com/story/2015/07/judge-explodes-over-hillary-email-delays-120804#ixzz3lRYN42fh.
[5] *Id.*
[6] Landmark Legal Found. v. EPA, 2015 U.S. Dist. LEXIS 24620 (D.D.C. Mar. 2, 2015).
[7] *Id.*
[8] Dep't of Justice, *Summary of Agency Chief FOIA Officer Reports for 2015 and Assessment of Agency Progress in Implementing the President's FOIA Memorandum and Attorney General Holder's FOIA Guidelines With OIP Guidance for Further Improvement* (2015); Nate Jones, *New DOJ FOIA Report an Exercise in "Grade Inflation;" Rewards some FOIA Denials as "Achieving Efficiencies"* Aug. 15, 2012, https://nsarchive.wordpress.com/2012/08/15/new-doj-foia-report-an-exercise-in-grade-inflation-rewards-some-foia-denials-as-increased-efficiencies/.

The Freedom of Information Act established a right for the public to access federal agency records. The statute simply requires requesters to reasonably describe the records they wish to receive and the agency is required to produce those records in 20 working days.[9] In practice, however, the FOIA process is much more complicated and difficult to navigate. Many of the complications are engineered into the process by the federal agencies themselves.

The FOIA process is broken. Unnecessary complications, misapplication of the law, and extensive delays are common occurrences. Agencies fail to articulate reasons for delays or explain how to navigate the process. Requesters wait months, not weeks, before receiving any response. Even a denial on a technicality can be significantly delayed because the agency may fail to read the request for months. Unreasonable requests for detail and repeated ultimatums to respond within narrow windows or start all over reinforce the perspective that the process is designed to keep out all but the most persistent and experienced requesters.

The Administration's Culture of Secrecy Erodes Trust

On January 21, 2009, President Obama issued an executive memorandum on FOIA, which stated:

> The Freedom of Information Act should be administered with a clear presumption: In the face of doubt, openness prevails. The Government should not keep information confidential merely because public officials might be embarrassed by disclosure, because errors and failures might be revealed, or because of speculative or abstract fears. Nondisclosure should never be based on an effort to protect the personal interests of Government officials at the expense of those they are supposed to serve. In responding to requests under the FOIA, executive branch agencies (agencies) should act promptly and in a spirit of cooperation, recognizing that such agencies are servants of the public. [10]

Less than four months later, however, the White House Counsel wrote a nonpublic memorandum reminding all Executive Branch agencies of the disclosure policy the Administration expected the agencies to observe in practice: all documents and records that implicate the White House in any way are said to have "White House equities" and must receive an extra layer of review, not by agency FOIA experts, but by the White House itself.[11]

---

[9] 5 U.S.C. § 552(a)(6)(A)(i).

[10] Memorandum from President Barack Obama for the Heads of Exec. Departments & Agencies, *Freedom of Information Act*, (Jan. 21, 2009).

[11] Memorandum from Gregory Craig, Counsel to the President, for all Exec. Dep't & Agency General Counsels, *Reminder Regarding Document Requests* (Apr. 15, 2009), *available at* http://causeofaction.org/assets/uploads/2013/06/White-House-memo-equities.pdf?92f52c.

At a June 2015 hearing, FOIA officers from multiple agencies confirmed that this policy
requiring White House review of certain documents remains in effect.[12] Despite a public
assertion that agencies should promptly respond and that the disclosure decision should not be
based on personal interests, on direction from the White House, agencies routinely delay
responses to allow for an extra layer of review by those persons with the greatest concerns about
embarrassment and revealing failures.

It is unclear how the White House equities consultation policy would further the
President's stated policy that "openness prevails" or how the policy would prevent nondisclosure
based on efforts to protect the personal interests of government officials. However, a record
obtained by the AP shows a redaction that sheds light on one of the policy's results. The
National Archives and Records Administration FOIA office staff redacted this sentence in every
case, except once, by mistake: "We live in constant fear of upsetting the WH (White House)."[13]
The statement is a simple and clear reminder about the chilling effect that White House
involvement in the FOIA process can have on agencies.

Political review fosters mistrust, causes delays, and invites malfeasance

Evidence shows political involvement in the FOIA process does not end at the White
House. Political officials at the Department of Homeland Security (DHS), the Department of
State, and the Department of Justice (DOJ) have interfered with the release of documents. In
multiple cases brought to the Committee's attention, FOIA requests were subjected to an
additional layer of review for political purposes and documents deemed problematic or
embarrassing were withheld from release. Politicizing the FOIA process places decisions about
the release of documents in the hands of officials with an insufficient knowledge of FOIA,

---

[12] H. Comm on Oversight & Gov't Reform, Subcomm. on Info. Tech. and Subcomm. on Gov't Operations,
Ensuring Agency Compliance with Freedom of Information Act (FOIA), 114th Cong. (2015).
[13] Associated Press, Press Release, *AP CEO: Gov't undermining 'right to know' laws,* Mar. 13, 2015,
http://www.ap.org/Content/Press-Release/2015/Gary-Pruitt-Sunshine-Week-column.

causing information to be wrongly withheld from the public. This practice wastes valuable agency time and resources while the backlog continues to grow.

Department of Homeland Security

The Department of Homeland Security receives the largest number of FOIA requests in the Federal government—more than 40 percent of all requests received in FY 2014. The Department is also responsible for the largest backlog of requests, about two-thirds of all backlogged requests.[14] DHS has maintained these distinctions since 2008, when it surpassed the Department of Veterans Affairs in both counts.[15] Given the burden to the agency, its inability to meet legal requirements, and the substantial inconvenience to the public, DHS should have been focused on finding efficiencies and ensuring prompt responses.

Instead, a 2011 investigation by the Committee found DHS leadership actually imposed additional procedural requirements that "corrupted the agency's FOIA compliance procedures, exerted political pressure on FOIA compliance officers, and undermined the federal government's accountability to the American people."[16] Under DHS's process, all significant FOIA requests were forwarded to the Secretary's political staff for review. Career FOIA experts could not release responses without the political staff's approval. Political staff lacking FOIA expertise proposed their own redactions and prevented the release of embarrassing information. DHS also abused the (b)(5) exemption, meant to protect predecisional records, to improperly withhold information. The Committee found that this layer of political review harmed the career FOIA staff's morale and delayed response times.[17]

Department of State

The Department of State is arguably the worst agency with respect to FOIA compliance.[18] The Agency has numerous open requests that are nearly a decade old. State takes months to process simple requests, and nearly a year for more complex cases that qualify for expedited treatment.[19] Recently, State has also faced increased FOIA litigation, much of which surrounds the record keeping practices of former Secretary Hillary Clinton and her senior staff.[20]

According to the *Wall Street Journal,* Secretary Clinton's senior staff "scrutinized politically sensitive documents requested under public records law and sometimes blocked their

---

[14] U.S. Dep't of Justice, *Summary of Annual FOIA Reports for Fiscal Year 2014* (May 5, 2015).

[15] U.S. Dep't of Justice, *FOIA Post (2009) Summary of Annual FOIA Reports for Fiscal Year 2008 available at* http://www.justice.gov/oip/blog/foia-post-2009-summary-annual-foia-reports-fiscal-year-2008 (last visited September 15, 2015).

[16] H. Comm. on Oversight & Gov't Reform, *Staff Report: A New Era of Openness?: How and Why Political Staff at DHS Interfered with the FOIA Process,* 112th Cong. (Mar. 30, 2011).

[17] *Id.*

[18] Chris Moody, *Report: Clinton State Dept one of least transparent agencies,* CNN, March 10, 2015 http://www.cnn.com/2015/03/10/politics/state-department-transparency-hillary-clinton/.

[19] Department of State, *Freedom of Information Act Annual Report Fiscal Year 2014* (2014).

[20] Josh Gerstein, *State Department cites 'crushing' burden from Freedom of Information Act* POLITICO, Apr. 2, 2015, http://www.politico.com/blogs/under-the-radar/2015/04/state-department-cites-crushing-burden-from-freedom-of-information-act-204948.

release."[21] Secretary Clinton's Chief of Staff, Cheryl Mills, and her staff reportedly screened documents requested about the Keystone XL pipeline and former President Bill Clinton's speaking engagements and in both cases withheld the release of some documents. According to the *Journal*, after Ms. Mills began reviewing documents related to Keystone XL, State's disclosure of records about the pipeline "fell off sharply."[22] Political appointees reportedly exerted a degree of influence that the Department's FOIA staff found inappropriate, including having a FOIA expert advise them on how to "prospectively shield documents from disclosure."[23]

Compounding concerns about inappropriate political review, State also has numerous high profile cases wherein the agency claimed there were no responsive records when documents did exist.[24] In a recent example, State reversed its initial claim in a 2013 FOIA case that the agency had no responsive records, having subsequently found more than 17,000 likely responsive records.[25] In 2013, Gawker, a media organization, filed a request with State for records between Philippe Reines, former Deputy Assistant Secretary of State for Strategic Communications under Clinton, and several dozen media outlets.[26] While the initial claim by State was incorrect, as Reines had well-documented communications with reporters, State did not identify any records until after Gawker invested the time and money required to take the Agency to court.[27]

A recent report from State's Office of the Inspector General revealed why State has not been producing these responsive documents.[28] As a matter of course, State did not search for them. According to the OIG, the FOIA analyst responsible for searching for records from the Secretary of State, the Deputy Secretaries of State, and many other high level political staff "described the decision to search email accounts to be a discretionary one that is only exercised periodically."[29] The periodic search for emails was only conducted if a request explicitly referred to "emails" or "all records."[30] If a request included those magic words, the FOIA analyst would ask State employees to search their own records and accept whatever was sent in response, without approving a search methodology or the results.[31]

---

[21] Laura Meckler, *Hillary Clinton's State Department Staff Kept Tight Rein on Records*, WALL ST. J., May 19, 2015, http://www.wsj.com/articles/hillary-clintons-state-department-staff-kept-tight-rein-on-records-1432081701.
[22] *Id.*
[23] *Id.*
[24] *See e.g.*, Erik Wemple, *More on Jason Leopold's crazy FOIA bind*, WASH. POST, June 4, 2015, https://www.washingtonpost.com/blogs/erik-wemple/wp/2015/06/04/more-on-jason-leopolds-crazy-foia-bind/; *see also* Josh Gerstein, *Sullivan, Mills turn over emails to State Department* POLITICO, July 8, 2015, http://www.politico.com/blogs/under-the-radar/2015/04/state-department-cites-crushing-burden-from-freedom-of-information-act-204948.
[25] J.K. Trotter, *State Department Finds Thousands of Phillipe Reines Emails It Claimed Did Not Exist*, GAWKER, Aug. 17, 2015, http://gawker.com/state-department-finds-thousands-of-philippe-reines-ema-1724560491.
[26] *Id.*
[27] *Id.*
[28] U.S. Dep't of State Office of the Inspector General, *Evaluation of the Department of State's FOIA Processes for Requests Involving the Office of the Secretary* (January 6, 2016).
[29] *Id.*
[30] *Id.*
[31] *Id.*

The Department of Justice is responsible for both FOIA requests submitted to DOJ and FOIA requests submitted across the federal government. The agency's Office of Information Policy (OIP) is supposed to be charged with ensuring compliance and implementation of FOIA law and policy.[32] The office publishes a comprehensive legal treatise addressing all aspects of FOIA. Given DOJ's expertise on the law and special role in enforcement, deviations from the letter and spirit of FOIA are even more troubling.

Yet, Justice Department has deliberately violated the FOIA statute's time requirements in the face of political concerns. In the wake of a General Services Administration (GSA) scandal regarding excessive and wasteful conference spending, many wondered whether similarly outrageous events occurred at other agencies. Cause of Action, a nonprofit organization, submitted FOIA requests to several agencies in April 2012 requesting documents related to purchases of commemorative and promotional items, one of the many areas of waste cited in the GSA scandal.[33]

Among the agencies questioned by Cause of Action, DOJ's delayed response stood out compared to other, more responsive, agencies. To understand the cause of the delay, Cause of Action submitted another FOIA request to DOJ, requesting records about the response to their original FOIA request. Documents produced in response to the second request show high-level discussions at DOJ in May 2012 regarding how to respond to the inquiries into spending.[34] DOJ component agencies received instructions to "stand down."[35] Component agencies finally received "the green light to send out the [ ] response" in November 2012, after much of the public outcry surrounding the GSA scandal had subsided.[36]

While the current Administration claims that it is "the most transparent administration in history," the evidence indicates otherwise.[37] As these cases show, political staff and agency employees strategize to avoid disclosure and transparency. Many groups and individuals have been denied records they have a right to access. These stories rightfully cause the public to wonder what the federal government is trying to hide. Secrecy fosters distrust.

The Executive Branch Has Adopted An Unlawful Presumption In Favor Of Secrecy

Testifying before the Committee, David McCraw, Assistant General Counsel for the New York Times, aptly described the central problem facing FOIA requesters:

---

[32] U.S. Dep't of Justice, *About the Office, available at* http://www.justice.gov/oip/about-office (last accessed September 15, 2015).
[33] Cause of Action, *FOIA Freak-Out: DOJ Scrambles to Avoid Fallout Over Swag Purchases*, Apr. 25, 2013, http://causeofaction.org/foia-freak-out-doj-scrambles-to-avoid-fallout-over-swag-purchases/.
[34] *Id.*
[35] *Id.*
[36] *Id.*
[37] Jonathan Easley, *Obama Says His is 'Most Transparent Administration' Ever*, THE HILL, Feb. 14, 2013, http://thehill.com/blogs/blog-briefing-room/news/283335-obama-this-is-the-most-transparent-administration-in-history.

First, much of the delay appears to have little to do with the nature and complexity of actual requests but instead results from a culture of unresponsiveness. Some agencies are consistently good, while others show little sign of improvement year after year. As requesters, we are not in a position to know what the root causes of delay are. . . .In the end, this is a management issue, and those in charge of agencies should be held accountable for figuring out what the problem is and fixing it.[38]

Agencies are responsible for distributing appropriate resources to the FOIA offices, including a sufficient number of personnel. For this reason, it is primarily the agencies themselves fostering a culture of responsiveness or unresponsiveness. Far too often, agencies have adopted a unlawful presumption in favor of secrecy when responding to Freedom of Information Act requests. While other agencies cited a lack of resources to excuse poor performance, the Chief FOIA Officer at the Department of Treasury, Brodi Fontenot, explained that Treasury prioritizes FOIA operations.[39] In 2013, Treasury doubled the staff in the FOIA office with a goal to close the oldest cases and find efficiencies to improve on existing processes. Treasury's commitment to FOIA had already shown results in faster processing times, a reduced backlog, and the closing of more than a dozen of the oldest outstanding cases.

The Administration reinforces the presumption of secrecy by celebrating failed agencies. In 2015, DOJ issued a report assessing progress on implementing the administration's FOIA policies including agency grades on compliance with FOIA where many of the worst performing agencies actually received the highest scores.[40] By grading agencies on email usage and whether they post reports online as required by law, 72 percent of agencies obtained top scores on a category titled "steps taken to greater utilize technology."[41] In the category assessing implementation of the presumption of openness, an agency only needed to send staff to FOIA training and make at least one discretionary disclosure to receive the highest marks–75% of agencies met this low threshold.[42]

As an example of this grade inflation, State, which averages three times the statutory time limit to process even simple requests, received the highest or second highest scores in four of five categories.[43] In the fifth category, which tracked metrics that matter to requesters, State received the lowest score, with zeros in metrics including processing time for simple requests, decrease in backlog, and percentage of backlog to overall agency requests.[44]

---

[38] H. Comm on Oversight & Gov't Reform, *Ensuring Transparency through the Freedom of Information Act (FOIA)*, 114th Cong. (June 2, 2015) (Statement of David McCraw, Assistant General Counsel for the New York Times).

[39] H. Comm. on Oversight & Gov't Reform, *Ensuring Agency Compliance with Freedom of Information Act (FOIA)*, 114th Cong. (June 3, 2015) (Statement of Brodi Fontenot, Chief FOIA Officer, Department of the Treasury).

[40] Department of Justice, *Summary of Agency Chief FOIA Officer Reports for 2015 and Assessment of Agency Progress in Implementing the President's FOIA Memorandum and Attorney General Holder's FOIA Guidelines with OIP Guidance for Further Improvement* (2015).

[41] *Id.*

[42] *Id.*

[43] *Id.*

[44] *Id.*

Perhaps the worst example of this presumption of secrecy involves Jason Leopold, a reporter for Vice News and a request to the Department of Defense (DOD).[45] In 2014, Leopold filed three increasingly detailed requests to simply obtain the title of reports produced from 2009 through 2014 by an office within DOD from.[46] In 2009, DOD released a list of titles of the reports from the office covering the previous 20 years.[47] In response to each of the three requests for the titles of more recent reports, DOD denied the request, either summarily claiming that "no documents of the kind described in the request could be located," or alternatively that the request was too onerous. Forced to file a lawsuit to enforce his right to access records, Leopold received an offer to settle from DOD. DOD agreed to partially fill this request if he agreed to never file another request. In essence, DOD would partially comply with its legal obligations if Leopold agreed to forfeit his rights in perpetuity.[48]

Exemptions Are Abused

Cases like that of Jason Leopold, where federal agencies make repeated and extreme efforts to subvert the public's right to access records and fail to comply with legal responsibilities, damage the public's trust in both FOIA and in the government as a whole. Trust is vital to the FOIA process precisely because not all records are released and requesters are forced to rely on agencies to withhold records for proper reasons. Rightfully, certain sensitive information is shielded from public disclosure. The statute provides nine exemptions from FOIA's broad mandate for full and complete access to federal agency records.[49]

FOIA exemptions are intended to maintain reasonable protections for many categories of sensitive information such as classified documents, personal or private information, the release of which would only result in embarrassment or harm, and trade secrets or other confidential business information. The very nature of exemptions, however, creates an operational impediment to accountability by obscuring information the public could use to assess whether the exemptions were appropriately applied. This barrier to accountability is no small matter. Last year Federal agencies cited exemptions more than 550,000 times to withhold information related to nearly 220,000 requests.[50]

In applying exemptions, agencies must first determine whether information qualifies for an exemption and whether the agency will apply the exemption if the applicable exemption is discretionary. Then, agencies are obligated to follow a few simple rules in redacting or withholding information: (1) Responsiveness to the request is determined on a page-by-page

---

[45] H. Comm on Oversight & Gov't Reform, *Ensuring Transparency through the Freedom of Information Act,* 114th Cong. (June 2, 2015) (Statement of Jason Leopold, Reporter for Vice News).
[46] Erik Wemple, *Judge orders release of pentagon records in Jason Leopold FOIA Case,* WASH. POST, June 11, 2015, https://www.washingtonpost.com/blogs/erik-wemple/wp/2015/06/11/judge-orders-release-of-pentagon-records-in-jason-leopold-foia-case/.
[47] *Id.*
[48] *Id.*
[49] 5 U.S.C. § 552(b).
[50] Dep't of Justice, *Summary of Annual FOIA Reports for Fiscal Year 2014* (May 5 2015).

basis; (2) If any information on a page is responsive, the entire page should be provided;[51] (3) If any information on a page is exempt, any segregable portion must be released;[52] and (4) When an exemption is invoked, it must be identified and, if technologically feasible, the exemption should be identified at the place on the record where the redaction was made.[53]

When used properly, redactions are a meaningful way to provide the public with information while protecting against the release of details that would harm an interest protected by an exemption. In practice, however, the agencies applying the exemptions have an inherent conflict of interest. The agency making the decision to withhold information is also the agency with the most at stake if embarrassing or controversial information is released. Every time evidence of an agency's abuse of exemptions is uncovered, mistrust grows.

Under the Redactions: A Side-by-Side Look

During an investigation into the Federal Communications Commission (FCC), the Committee obtained two sets of nearly identical documents – one set of redacted documents obtained through FOIA requests and one set of unredacted documents obtained pursuant to a congressional request, to which the FOIA exemptions do not apply. The opportunity to look under the FOIA redactions was enlightening. More than 200 side-by-side examples are included in Appendix A.

Misapplication of exemption (b)(5)

In the documents released through FOIA, the FCC marked most of the redactions as "(b)(5)." Exemption five allows agencies to redact information that would be considered privileged in a legal proceeding, such as communications covered by the attorney-client privilege.[54] Agencies also enjoy a privilege called "deliberative process."

The deliberative process privilege protects the agency decision-making process by allowing the agency to withhold documents and communications that are (1) predecisional and (2) deliberative.[55] Predecisional means the material must have been created prior to the adoption of a policy.[56] Deliberative means that the materials contain recommendations or express opinions on legal or policy matters.[57]

---

[51] Dep't of Justice, *FOIA Update: OIP Guidance: Determining the Scope of a FOIA Request* (Jan. 1, 1995), *available at* http://www.justice.gov/oip/blog/foia-update-oip-guidance-determining-scope-foia-request [hereinafter Dep't of Justice, *FOIA Update*]. Essentially, this means that agencies should not redact material as "nonresponsive." Any document provided in response to a FOIA request should not contain any redactions that do not qualify for an exemption.

[52] 5 U.S.C. § 552(b).

[53] 5 U.S.C. § 552(b).

[54] Dept. of Justice, *Guide to Freedom of Information Act: Exemption 5*, *available at* http://www.justice.gov/sites/default/files/oip/legacy/2014/07/23/exemption5.pdf (last accessed Sept. 24, 2015).

[55] *Id.*

[56] *Id.*

[57] *Id.*

The (b)(5) exemption, which has come to be known as the "withhold it because you want to" exemption, is frequently misapplied.[58] The FCC documents demonstrate the misapplication of exemption five. For example, this January 6, 2014 email—provided to a FOIA requester—is fully redacted pursuant to exemption (b)(5):[59]

-----Original Message-----
From: Philip Verveer
Sent: Monday, January 06, 2014 1:05 PM
To: Justin Cole; Ruth Milkman; Renee Gregory; Daniel Alvarez; Jonathan Sallet; Gigi Sohn; Neil Grace; Sara Morris; Patrick Halley; Shannon Gilson; Mark Wigfield; Stephanie Weiner; Roger Sherman; Julie Veach
Subject: RE: AT&T rollout of sponsored data service at CES

(b) (5)

The unredacted version of the email, however, shows a post-decisional communication. The email refers to the Chairman having already "approved" language for a speech. Thus, this document was created after the decision was made and cannot be withheld pursuant to the "deliberative process" privilege. The unredacted version states:[60]

-----Original Message-----
From: Philip Verveer
Sent: Monday, January 06, 2014 1:05 PM
To: Justin Cole; Ruth Milkman; Renee Gregory; Daniel Alvarez; Jonathan Sallet; Gigi Sohn; Neil Grace; Sara Morris; Patrick Halley; Shannon Gilson; Mark Wigfield; Stephanie Weiner; Roger Sherman; Julie Veach
Subject: RE: AT&T rollout of sponsored data service at CES

This is the language that TW has requested and approved for the Silicon Valley speech:

"The necessity for these policies [FCC oversight and the ability to intervene] and the wisdom of case specific approaches to implementing them is demonstrated by a coincidental occurrence earlier this week. AT&T announced a mobile service offering that enables subscribing firms to cover the airtime costs of accessing their content. Based in part on the premise that mobile service is competitive, the

In another instance, the FCC redacted an April 29, 2014 email from an unknown individual to several individuals on the President's staff:[61]

---

[58] National Security Archive, *The Next FOIA Fight: The B(5) "Withhold It Because You Want To" Exemption*, Mar. 27, 2014, https://nsarchive.wordpress.com/2014/03/27/the-next-foia-fight-the-b5-withold-it-because-you-want-to-exemption/.
[59] Email from Phillip Verveer to Justin Cole, *et al.* (Jan. 6, 2014, 1:05 p.m.) (redacted).
[60] Email from Phillip Verveer to Justin Cole, *et al.* (Jan. 6, 2014, 1:05 p.m.) (unredacted).
[61] Email from [REDACTED BY FCC] to Jeff Zientz, *et al.* (Apr. 29, 2014, 7:52 p.m.) (redacted).

From:

Sent: Tuesday, April 29, 2014 7:52 PM

To: 'Jeff Zientz'; 'Jason Furman'; 'Tom Power'; 'John D. Podesta'

Subject: Open Internet update

Attachments: NCTA Final4-29.docx

Gentlemen –

Below is the link to today's blog further explaining the Open Internet NPRM (b) (5)

Attached is my speech to NCTA tomorrow (b) (5)

T

Even from the redacted email, it is readily apparent the redactions are inappropriate. The subject line calls the email an "update" and the unredacted portions reference final documents. The redaction of the sender's name—known from another version of the email to be FCC Chairman Tom Wheeler—is particularly egregious.

The unredacted version confirms that Chairman Wheeler is simply reiterating prior statements or providing summaries of existing public documents. The Chairman does comment on his perception of the reaction from the press. However, that opinion does not address policy or legal opinions.[62]

Perhaps more importantly, the FCC has insisted that the White House was not part of the deliberative process. Chairman Wheeler compared the White House's comments to those of

---

[62] *See* Elec. Frontier Found. v. DOJ, 826 F. Supp. 2d 157, 169 (D.D.C. 2011) (denying exemption 5 protection to emails summarizing factual matters and not relating to formation of policy); CREW v. DHS, 648 F. Supp. 2d 152, 160 (D.D.C. 2011) (requiring release of portion of memorandum not discussing policy).

Members from Congress, calling them "recommendations."[63] Redacting a description of the President's opinion on this issue, as the version of the email released under FOIA does, is improper. The (b)(5) exemption only covers documents that reflect "the give-and-take of the consultative process."[64] The unredacted version of the email states:[65]

From:	TW
Sent:	Tuesday, April 29, 2014 7:52 PM
To:	'Jeff Zientz'; 'Jason Furman'; 'Tom Power'; 'John D. Podesta'
Subject:	Open Internet update
Attachments:	NCTA Final4-29.docx

Gentlemen -

Below is the link to today's blog further explaining the Open Internet NPRM. The press reaction has been what we'd hoped, that I have clarified previous misconceptions about how the proposal would somehow gut the Open Internet.

Attached is my speech to NCTA tomorrow. The first two pages are about Open Internet - a message delivered to the broadband providers as to what will be expected.

Message in both: (1) it is a proposal on which we seek comment, (2) all options are on the table, including Title II, and (3) I have flat out expressed skepticism that we'd find "commercial reasonableness" to be a route to exceptions to the rule for special deals and prioritization.

As I have said since February, the proposal is designed to deliver on the goals of the 2010 Open Internet Order (which, you'll recall, included a reasonableness test) and to do so in a manner that follows the D.C. Circuit's roadmap (and hopefully thus avoids litigation).

The President has supported the Open Internet and anti-discrimination. Just like he supported the 2010 order with its reasonableness test there is no need to no change with this proposal. I believe he can say that we are using current law to its fullest (and in a manner that was prescribed by the court) to assure an Open Internet and anti-discrimination. The next step is to change the law, even Title II has a "just and reasonable" test.

Hope this is helpful.

The initial coverage has been helpful and the feedback from the public interest groups better. I'll send you some clips in a moment.

T

Finally, the FCC redacted a discussion surrounding a response to a press inquiry under the (b)(5) exemption. Courts are split on whether or not discussions peripheral to the development of policy are covered under exemption five. Even if these types of discussions are covered, however, the final decision is not. Further, the FCC redacted even non-substantive

---

[63] H. Comm. on Oversight & Gov't Reform, *Hearing on FCC: Process & Transparency*, 114th Cong. (Mar. 17, 2015).

[64] Coastal States Gas Corp. v. Dep't of Energy, 617 F.2d 854, 867 (D.C. Cir. 1980).

[65] Email from Hon. Thomas Wheeler, Chairman, FCC, to Jeff Zientz, *et al.* (Apr. 29, 2014, 7:52 p.m.) (unredacted).

communications. All of the text of the email chain is redacted from the version released by the FCC under FOIA:[66]

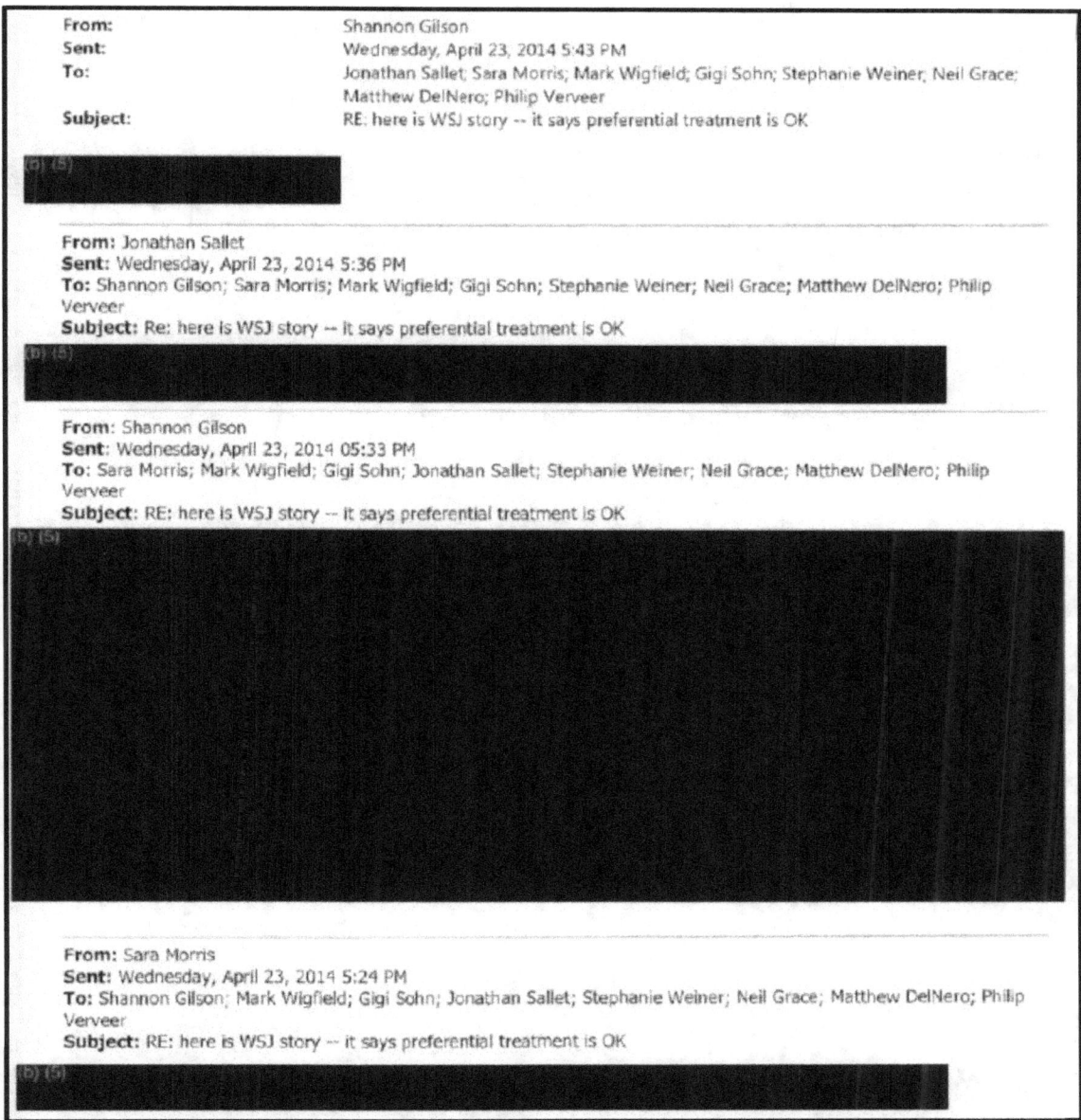

From: Shannon Gilson
Sent: Wednesday, April 23, 2014 5:43 PM
To: Jonathan Sallet; Sara Morris; Mark Wigfield; Gigi Sohn; Stephanie Weiner; Neil Grace; Matthew DelNero; Philip Verveer
Subject: RE: here is WSJ story -- it says preferential treatment is OK

(b) (5)

From: Jonathan Sallet
Sent: Wednesday, April 23, 2014 5:36 PM
To: Shannon Gilson; Sara Morris; Mark Wigfield; Gigi Sohn; Stephanie Weiner; Neil Grace; Matthew DelNero; Philip Verveer
Subject: Re: here is WSJ story -- it says preferential treatment is OK

(b) (5)

From: Shannon Gilson
Sent: Wednesday, April 23, 2014 05:33 PM
To: Sara Morris; Mark Wigfield; Gigi Sohn; Jonathan Sallet; Stephanie Weiner; Neil Grace; Matthew DelNero; Philip Verveer
Subject: RE: here is WSJ story -- it says preferential treatment is OK

(b) (5)

From: Sara Morris
Sent: Wednesday, April 23, 2014 5:24 PM
To: Shannon Gilson; Mark Wigfield; Gigi Sohn; Jonathan Sallet; Stephanie Weiner; Neil Grace; Matthew DelNero; Philip Verveer
Subject: RE: here is WSJ story -- it says preferential treatment is OK

(b) (5)

The unredacted email states:[67]

---

[66] Email from Shannon Gilson to Jonathan Sallet, *et al.* (Apr. 23, 2014 5:43 p.m.) (redacted).
[67] Email from Shannon Gilson to Jonathan Sallet, *et al.* (Apr. 23, 2014 5:43 p.m.) (redacted).

The email at 5:24 p.m. discusses possible edits. However, the 5:33 p.m. email contains the final language and at 5:43 p.m. that final language became public. Even if this type of discussion would be covered under exemption five, by 5:33 p.m. the decision had been made and the exemption was no longer applicable. Thus, the emails after 5:33 p.m. should not have been withheld under the (b)(5) exemption.

Agencies must determine responsiveness to the request on a page-by-page basis. If any information on a page falls within the scope of the request, then the entire page should be provided.[68] On numerous occasions, however, the FCC made "non-responsive" redactions.

In one example, the entire top portion of a document is redacted as being apparently non-responsive:[69]

Non-responsive

From: Susan Fisenne
Sent: Wednesday, January 15, 2014 11:17 AM
To: EDOCSHELP
Cc: Sharon Hurd; Courtney Reinhard
Subject: RE: Doc ID 325120 O'Rielly's item on Net Neutrality. Thanks.

Good morning,

There is a typo in Commissioner O'Rielly's statement on Net Neutrality. The attached version is correct. Will you please replace his net neutrality statement on the web with the attached corrected version?

Thank you so much and thanks Sharon for the catch!
Susan

---

[68] Dep't of Justice, *FOIA Update, supra* note 21. Essentially, this means that agencies should not redact material as "nonresponsive." Any document provided in response to a FOIA request should not contain any redactions that do not qualify for an exemption.

[69] Email from Susan Fisenne to EDOCSHELP (Jan. 15, 2014, 11:17 a.m.) (redacted).

The unredacted version of the document shows that not only is there no reason to withhold this from the requester, but that the redacted email is likely responsive. The email simply confirmed that the correct document on Net Neutrality had been replaced:[70]

From:	Bryan Payne on behalf of EDOCSHELP
Sent:	Wednesday, January 15, 2014 11:32 AM
To:	Susan Fisenne; EDOCSHELP
Cc:	Sharon Hurd; Courtney Reinhard
Subject:	RE: Doc ID 325120 O'Rielly's item on Net Neutrality. Thanks.
Follow Up Flag:	Follow up
Flag Status:	Flagged

Hi Susan,

Doc. 325120 has been replaced.

Sure Thing!
Bryan Payne
OMD/OSEC/IRG
Information Systems Support Specialist
202.418.0925

From: Susan Fisenne
Sent: Wednesday, January 15, 2014 11:17 AM
To: EDOCSHELP
Cc: Sharon Hurd; Courtney Reinhard
Subject: RE: Doc ID 325120 O'Rielly's item on Net Neutrality. Thanks.

Good morning,

There is a typo in Commissioner O'Rielly's statement on Net Neutrality. The attached version is correct. Will you please replace his net neutrality statement on the web with the attached corrected version?

Thank you so much and thanks Sharon for the catch!
Susan

Additional examples of agency redaction of non-responsive information can be found in Appendix A.

Inappropriate (b)(6) redactions

Exemption six applies to documents that "would constitute a clearly unwarranted invasion of privacy."[71] Exemption six requires the agency to balance the privacy interest against

---

[70] Email from Susan Fisenne to EDOCSHELP (Jan. 15, 2014, 11:17 a.m.) (unredacted to show top email).

the public interest in disclosure. Civilian, non-law enforcement personnel generally have no expectation of privacy regarding their names, titles, grades, salaries, and other information.

Without explanation, the FCC redacts the Chairman's initials under a (b)(6) exemption. Every time "TW" appears in the address line of an email it is redacted. Examples of the redactions that are applied to the Chairman's initials are circled in red, below. In this example, the Chairman's email address is redacted, while the contact information for the third party contacting the Chairman was completely unredacted. The Committee applied redactions to this document that cover telephone numbers and other contact information that the FCC did not redact. Those redactions are in blue, below. The version of the email released by the FCC under FOIA included significant redactions:[72]

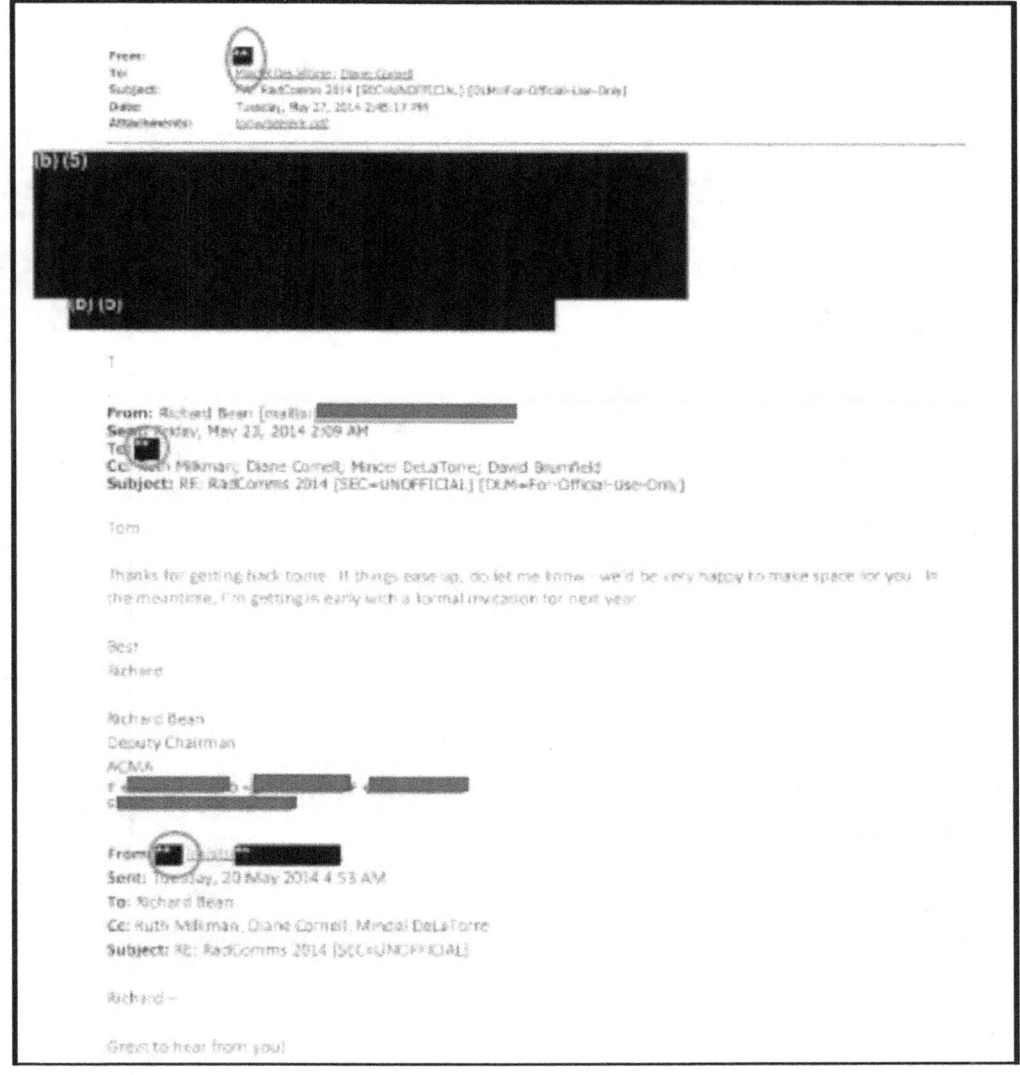

---

[71] Dep't of Justice, *Guide to Freedom of Information Act: Exemption 6*, available at http://www.justice.gov/sites/default/files/oip/legacy/2014/07/23/exemption6.pdf (last accessed Sept. 24, 2015).
[72] Email from [REDACTED BY FCC] to Mindel De LaTorre, and Diane Cornell (May 27, 2014 at 2:45:17 PM) (redacted).

The unredacted email shows that the FCC redacted the Chairman's initials, "TW," from the sender line of the emails three times. It is unclear why FCC has determined that releasing the initials of the top agency official acting his official capacity is a "clearly unwarranted invasion of privacy." What is clear, however, is that FCC is not appropriately balancing the public interest in disclosure. The requester receiving these documents would have no way of knowing the Chairman's involvement. This stands in contrast to the other Commissioners and numerous FCC staff whose names are not redacted. The unredacted email states:[73]

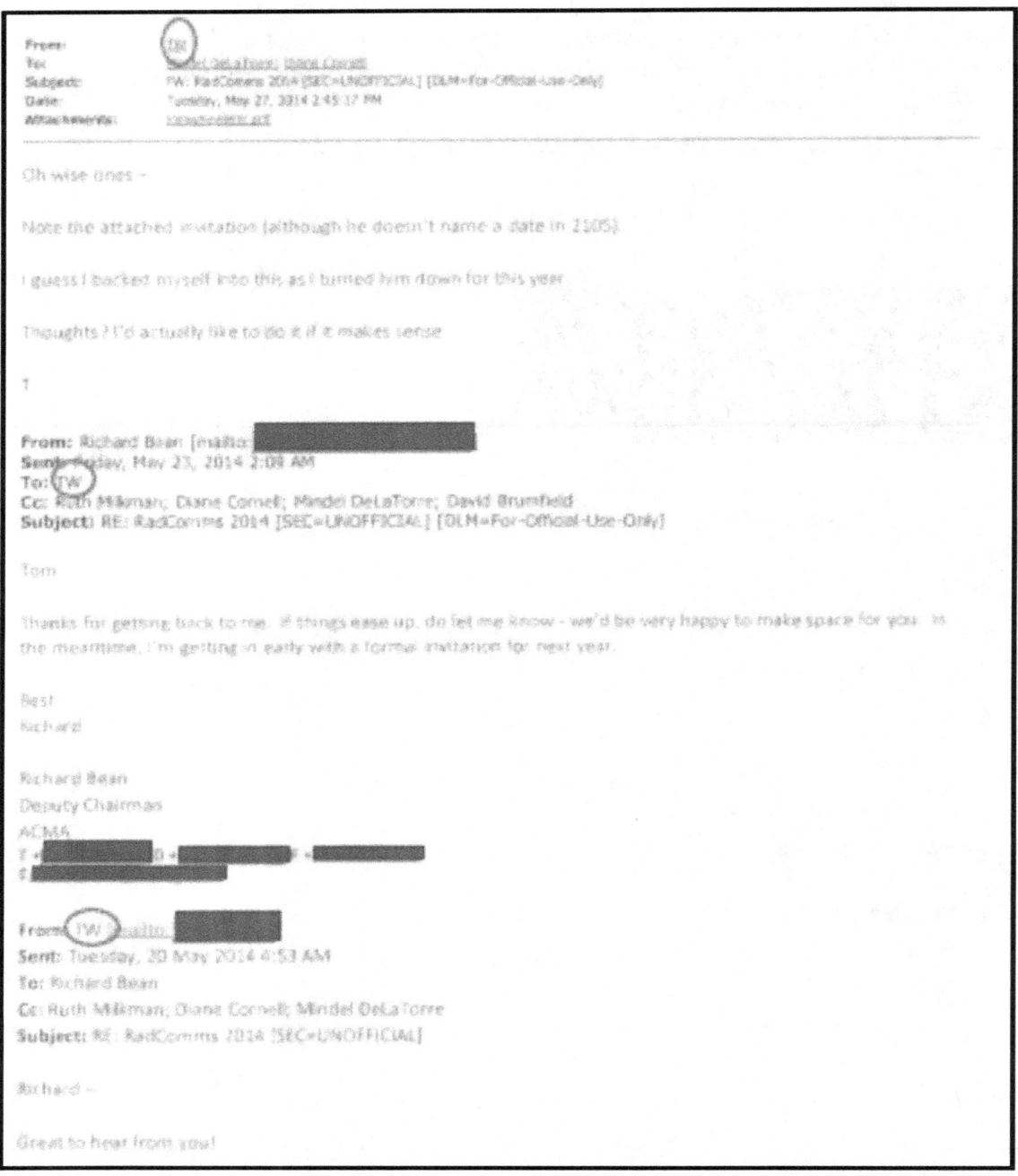

---

[73] Email from Hon. Thomas Wheeler, Chairman, FCC to Mindel De LaTorre, and Diane Cornell (May 27, 2014 at 2:45:17 PM) (redacted).

The FCC also applied the (b)(5) exemption to an email from the Chairman discussing an invitation to a conference. While the discussion was perhaps prior to the decision of whether the Chairman would attend, it does not appear to involve any predecisional discussion of a policy matter.

Numerous examples of the FCC redactions of the Chairman's initials, which appear near unredacted contact information for third parties, including members of the media, are included in Appendix A.

The FCC's tendency to over-redact makes it difficult for requesters to understand what the agency has provided them, and consequently, to make follow up requests. For example, in response to a request from Vice News reporter Jason Leopold, the FCC withheld 1,900 pages in their entirety under exemption five.[74] These redactions demonstrate a lack of responsiveness to the public's right for information. The agency either misunderstands how to use redactions, raising concerns of competency, or the agency intentionally misuses redactions, raising concerns of integrity. Given the numerous examples in which the FCC improperly redacts information, this may be a deliberate tactic to withhold information from the public.

More Stories of Ridiculous Redactions and Inappropriate Exemptions

The On-going Investigation of a Closed Case

On April 21, 2014, a federal officer shot and killed a defendant at federal courthouse in Salt Lake City, Utah.[75] The defendant, Siale Angilau, was on trial for "mafia-style racketeering charges," and was the last of 17 defendants in the case to stand trial.[76] When he rushed for a witness with a pen, a U.S. Marshal shot Angilau several times in the back.[77] Less than three months later, the Federal Bureau of Investigation (FBI) concluded its investigation into the event and closed the case.[78]

Months after the investigation had concluded, local media requested records from the U.S. Marshals Service (USMS) and the FBI relating to the shooting and investigation, including a courtroom video that captured the event on tape.[79] Every request was denied. The USMS claimed every responsive record was covered by either a privacy exemption or a law enforcement exemption.[80] Despite no open cases involving either two parties involved in the incident, USMS cited exemption (7)(a), which involves records "reasonably expected to interfere

---

[74] Letter from FCC to Jason Leopold, Vice News (Apr. 8, 2015).
[75] Ben Winslow and Kiersten Nunez, *Accused gang member dies in federal courthouse shooting*, FOX13, Apr. 21, 2015, http://fox13now.com/2014/04/21/shots-fired-in-federal-courthouse/.
[76] Associated Press, *No charges for marshal in Utah courtroom shooting*, CNS NEWS, July 15, 2014, http://cnsnews.com/news/article/no-charges-marshal-utah-courtroom-shooting.
[77] *Id.*
[78] *Id.*
[79] Email from Nate Carlisle, Salt Lake Trib. to U.S. Marshals Serv. FOIA (Sept. 5, 2014).
[80] Letter from U.S. Marshals Serv. to Nate Carlisle, Salt Lake Trib. (Sept. 24. 2014).

with enforcement proceedings" if disclosed. Incredulously, the FBI was unable to find even one responsive record.[81] Faced with denials, the requesters may now consider whether to pursue this further through litigation.

Food and Drug Administration Redacts Curriculum Vitae

In 2014, Public Citizen, a nonprofit organization, submitted a FOIA request to the Food and Drug Administration (FDA), asking for the curriculum vitae (CV) of the FDA's advisory committee members.[82] CVs are documents detailing an individual's professional accomplishments and commonly available online. Many of the FDA's advisory committee members' CVs are posted on the FDA's website, but they include redactions. According to Public Citizen, 80 to 100 percent of the CVs available online were redacted. [83]

When FDA provided records responsive to the request, the CVs remained redacted. Redactions included information such as publicly available professional license numbers, publication names, grant amounts, and past work history.[84] FDA noted some redactions as (b)(4), exempting trade secrets and confidential commercial information, and others as (b)(6), exempting information the disclosure of which would constitute an unwarranted invasion of privacy.[85] Public Citizen explained, "the notion that a rational person would include on her CV information 'the disclosure of which would constitute a clearly unwarranted invasion of personal privacy,' as required to meet the exemption 6 standard, is hard to fathom."[86]

DOJ Redacts the Titles of Office of Legal Counsel Opinions and the Names of Authors

In December 2012, Ryan Reilly, a Huffington Post reporter, made a FOIA request to DOJ, asking for the Office of Legal Counsel (OLC) to provide a list of all of the opinions it had issued during the Obama administration.[87] In response to the request, the OLC sent a heavily redacted list for the years 2009 through the beginning of 2013 that included 76 unclassified opinions.[88] Many titles were fully redacted while others were partially redacted. When DOJ provided Mr. Reilly the list of 10 unclassified OLC opinions from 2013, DOJ fully redacted the titles of all but one, and partially redacted the last title.[89] DOJ classified the full redactions as

---

[81] Letter from U.S. Dep't of Justice to Nate Carlisle, Salt Lake Trib. (July 28, 2014).
[82] Letter from Public Citizen to H. Comm. on Oversight & Gov't Reform (May 19, 2015) [hereinafter Public Citizen].
[83] *Id.*
[84] *Id.*
[85] 5 U.S.C. § 552(b).
[86] Public Citizen, *supra* note 28.
[87] Ryan Reilly, *Obama Justice Department Won't Disclose Number of Classified OLC Opinions* (UPDATE), HUFFINGTON POST, Feb. 25, 2013, http://www.huffingtonpost.com/2013/02/25/obama-classified-olc-opinions_n_2759878.html.
[88] *Id.* The response also noted the existence of eleven lists of classified OLC opinions that would not be provided, with no indication of the number of opinions included on these lists..
[89] Ryan J. Reilly, Tweet (Apr. 24, 2014, 8:12 a.m.), *available at* https://twitter.com/ryanjreilly/status/459349265916395520/photo/1 (last accessed Sept. 24, 2015).

(b)(5) exemptions, which covers legal privileges including attorney client privilege or deliberative process privilege, but failed to specify which legal privilege applied.[90]

For some of the partially redacted titles of OLC opinions, DOJ redacted the name of the author under a (b)(6) exemption, claiming that identifying the author "would constitute a clearly unwarranted invasion of the personal privacy of third parties."[91] According to a DOJ memo discussing OLC's purpose, "[OLC] is frequently asked to opine on issues of first impression that are unlikely to be resolved by the courts—a circumstance in which OLC's advice may effectively be the final word on the controlling law."[92] It is hard to imagine how identifying the federal employee who authored a legal memo which "may effectively be the final word on the controlling law" would "constitute a clearly unwarranted invasion of the personal privacy of [a] third part[y]." Further, the failure to redact some names makes the redaction of other names all the more curious.

Ph.D. Dissertation Materials Withheld by the Department of Energy

While it is never justifiable for the government to withhold information that the public is entitled to view, the practice becomes even more frustrating when the government prevents the release of an individual's own work. One example submitted to the Committee came from a Ph.D. candidate who had been working on his dissertation at Los Alamos National Lab when he was laid off. When the Ph.D. candidate tried to retrieve his work, he was told that he needed to file a FOIA request.[93]

After more than a year, the Department of Energy (DOE) partially granted, but largely denied the request under exemption (b)(2) of FOIA, claiming that "if any of the information was released, it could cause significant harm to the Agency's nuclear nonproliferation program[.]"[94]

Several months later, the Supreme Court clarified the application of (b)(2).[95] Striking down lower court opinions which found the exemption covered predominantly internal materials the disclosure of which would significantly risk circumvention of agency regulations or other law, the Court reaffirmed the statutory text. As the Court noted, (b)(2) contains "12 simple words: 'related solely to the internal personnel rules and practices of an agency'" and found that (b)(2) is intended to cover only employee relations and human resource matters.

The Ph.D. candidate subsequently filed an appeal. DOE reevaluated his request and claimed that the files had been properly withheld.[96] In 2011, after requesting a second appeal,

---

[90] Ryan J. Reilly, Tweet (July, 25, 2014, 10:45 a.m.), *available at* https://twitter.com/ryanjreilly/status/492727303592366083 (last accessed Sept. 24, 2015)..

[91] *Id.*

[92] Memorandum from David Barron, Acting Assistant Attorney Gen., U.S. Dep't of Justice, to Attorneys of the Office of Legal Counsel, *Best Practices for OLC Legal Advice & Written Opinions* (July 16, 2010).

[93] Email from Mr. Brener to the H. Comm. on Oversight & Gov't Reform, (May 13, 2015, 7:02PM). [Hereinafter "Brener"].

[94] Letter from Nat'l Nuclear Security Admin. to Mr. and Ms. Brener (Aug. 10, 2010)..

[95] Milner v. Dep't of the Navy, 131 S. Ct. 1259 (2011).

[96] Letter from Nat'l Nuclear Security Admin. to Mr. and Ms. Brener (Nov. 8, 2010).

DOE wrote to explain that his appeal request would be partially granted.[97] Four years later, DOE has yet to respond any further. The Ph.D. candidate's submission to the Committee also noted that the agency refused to even give him the "automatic Sudoku solver that [he] wrote."[98]

EPA Hides Conversation with Third Parties

In 2010, the National Shooting Sports Foundation, Inc. (NSSF) discovered that EPA and the American Bird Conservancy (ABC) engaged in conversations about the EPA's ability to regulate lead ammunition.[99] NSSF sent a FOIA request to EPA asking for documents related to the meeting between EPA and ABC, to which EPA responded that the information was protected by exemption (b)(5)—thereby claiming that the deliberative process and attorney client privileges protected the information.[100] EPA failed to explain how agency records relating to a discussion between the agency and an outside party could be covered under either the deliberative process privilege or the attorney client privilege.

NSSF subsequently appealed the denial and won, receiving partially redacted documents.[101] NSSF ultimately received the information it needed to determine whether EPA did in fact have conversations with ABC. Further, after seeing the unredacted information, NSSF better understand the partial exemptions as correctly protected under the deliberative and attorney client privileges. The EPA FOIA office's original decision to withhold the information in response to NSSF's request forced the parties into litigation simply to answer a very basic question. The EPA's decision to withhold the documents and litigate the release of those documents wasted time and resources, including taxpayer money.

Intra-Agency Consultation Wastes Resources and Causes Delays

It is common practice for agencies to consult with other agencies that may have "equities" in the documents requested.[102] Documents that either originated with another agency or contain information that is of interest to another agency are deemed to implicate that other agency's equities. The agency that received the FOIA request may choose to consult and obtain clearance from the other agency prior to release of such documents.[103] The consultation process is recognized in the statute, but current agency practice exceeds statutory time limits and can lead to extensive delays in responding to FOIA requests.[104]

---

[97] Letter from Nat'l Nuclear Security Admin. to Mr. Brener (May 20, 2011).

[98] Brener, *supra* note 39.

[99] A request for correspondence between EPA and ABC was included in the original FOIA request that NSSF made to EPA.

[100] Letter from Nat'l Shooting Sports Found. Political Action Comm. to EPA, (Oct. 10, 2011); Letter from EPA to Nat'l Shooting Sports Found., Inc., (Jan. 11, 2012).

[101] Letter from Sidley Austin LLP, to EPA (Feb. 9, 2012); Letter from EPA to Sidley Austin LLP (Mar. 14, 2012).

[102] Department of Justice, *Referrals, Consultations, and Coordination: Procedures for Processing Records When Another Agency or Entity Has an Interest in Them* (Aug. 15, 2014), *available at* http://www.justice.gov/oip/blog/foia-guidance-13 (last accessed Sept. 24, 2015).

[103] *Id.*

[104] 5 U.S.C. § 552

As a baseline, the FOIA statute provides agencies with twenty working days to respond to requesters with a determination regarding whether the agency will comply with a request.[105] Upon a determination from the agency that it will comply, the records are to be made promptly available.[106] Agency equities come into the process under what the statute describes as an "unusual circumstance."[107] The need for consultation is one of three unusual circumstances and the statute requires that the consultation be conducted with all practicable speed. Still, a finding that a case involves unusual circumstances provides only 10 additional days before a response is due. In many instances, agencies allow the consultation process to serve as an effective denial without officially making an adverse determination.

A Never Ending Consultation and Referral Process

As an example, on January 10, 2005 the National Security Archive submitted a FOIA request to the Department of Defense Inspector General (DOD-IG) for School of the Americas training manual evaluations.[108] The agency acknowledged receipt of the request three days later.[109] Nearly ten years later, on December 3, 2014, the DOD-IG finally made a determination.[110] DOD-IG released some documents, but withheld more than a thousand in their entirety, primarily under exemption (b)(6). The DOD-IG referred the remaining documents to fourteen different agencies to review and asked those fourteen separate agencies to respond directly to the National Security Archive.

The National Security Archive provided the Committee with the responses it had received from the fourteen agencies where its request was forwarded. The Air Force responded on January 9, 2015:[111]

---

[105] 5 U.S.C. § 552(a)(6).
[106] 5 U.S.C. § 552(a)(6).
[107] 5 U.S.C. § 552(a)(6).
[108] Letter from the Nat'l Sec. Archive to Inspector Gen., Dep't of Defense (Jan. 10, 2005).
[109] Letter from Freedom of Info. Act & Privacy Act Office, Office of the Inspector Gen., Dep't of Defense, to Thomas Blanton, Nat'l Sec. Archive (Jan. 13, 2005).
[110] Letter from Freedom of Info. & Privacy Office, Office of the Inspector Gen., Dep't of Defense, to Thomas Blanton, Nat'l Sec. Archive (Dec. 3, 2014).
[111] Letter from Dep't of the Air Force, Gov't Info. Specialist to Thomas Blanton, Nat'l Sec. Archive (Jan. 9, 2015).

This is in response to your, 1 October 2005 Department of Defense (DoD) Inspector General (IG) Freedom of Information Act request (Ref: 05-0112) and received in our office 15 December 2014 as a DoD IG referral. The request relates to Archives #20050014DOD005.

During the release of documents responsive to your request, DoD IG identified documents that belonged to the United States Air Force (USAF). DoD IG referred 227 pages that required review by the USAF prior to being released. This request has been assigned FOIA case number 2015-01759-F.

From this referral SAF/AAII (FOIA) identified three pages that required review from this office. This review was conducted by the Office of the General Counsel (SAF/GC).

SAF/GC completed a review of pages 190-192 from the file and determined that in accordance with Freedom of Information Act certain information should be withheld under Title 5 U.S.C. § 552 (b)(5). FOIA exemption (b)(5) protects attorney client privileged information. SAF/GC is the denial authority in this instance.

Additionally, the remaining 224 pages have been transferred to Air Combat Command (ACC) and Air Education and Training Command (AETC) for review. ACC was assigned FOIA Case #2015-01773-F for the review of page 174. AETC was assigned FOIA Case #2015-01774-F and will review the remaining 223 pages.

The DOD-IG forwarded the Air Force 227 pages. The Air Force FOIA office identified three pages that it would review. The FOIA office then transferred the remaining to two other component agencies, asking one agency to review one page and another agency to review the remaining 223 pages.

The National Security Archive continues to wait for responses to it 2005 request.

Delayed Referral Results in More Delay

Philip Eil, a freelance journalist based in Providence, Rhode Island, filed a FOIA request on February 1, 2012 with the Executive Office for U.S. Attorneys (EOUSA).[112] EOUSA confirmed its receipt of the FOIA request by the end of the month and then responded nine months later, in November 2012, to explain that EOUSA found records that "may or may not be responsive" but, because the records originated at another agency, EOUSA refused to process the records.[113] EOUSA transferred the request to the Drug Enforcement Agency (DEA) and charged

---

[112] Letter from Philip Eil to Executive Office for U.S. Attorneys (Feb. 1, 2012).
[113] Letter from Executive Office for U.S. Attorneys to Phil Eli [sic] (Feb. 28, 2012); Letter from Executive Office for U.S. Attorneys to Phil Eli [sic] (Nov. 29, 2012).

Mr. Eil a $154 "review fee."[114] As a journalist, Mr. Eil's fee category only obligates him to pay duplication costs.

More than two years later, Mr. Eil filed a lawsuit to compel DEA to fully respond and provide responsive documents without excessive redactions.[115] By the time Mr. Eli filed his suit, DEA had processed 12,724 pages, withholding 87 percent of those pages. The pages DEA did were stripped of most of the substantive information.[116] The lawsuit is ongoing.

"Frustratingly Slow Process"

The *New York Times* describes its experience with agency equities consultation as a "frustratingly slow process in which some agencies express no objection to the release of their agency names, some do, and some initially do but later reverse their decisions on appeal."[117] On July 5, 2013, the *New York Times* filed a FOIA request with the United States Postal Inspection Service (USPIS) seeking documents outlining the number of "mail covers," a law enforcement surveillance tool, requested by outside law enforcement agencies from 2001 to 2012.[118] On March 31, 2014, The *New York Times* prevailed in a FOIA appeal, and USPIS agreed to release the requested documents, subject to possible redactions based on opposition from other agencies.[119]

Fourteen months later, approximately two dozen agencies, including local agencies, agreed to release the requested information.[120] Then, on March 2, 2015, USPIS unilaterally decided (1) that it would no longer facilitate responses for data from state and local agencies that had requested federal mail covers, despite having done so at that point for nearly a year, and (2) that it would close the FOIA request and no longer actively pursue information from the remaining federal agencies because those agencies were taking a long time to respond to USPIS inquiries.[121] The *New York Times* appealed USPIS's decision and on April 28, 2015 the USPIS, without explanation, stated that it was reversing itself and would process the information as before.[122]

The *New York Times* explains that in the referral process, "[t]here is no incentive for the second agency to act quickly and no mechanism for ensuring a timely response. Meanwhile,

---

[114] *Id.*

[115] Complaint, Eil v. U.S. Drug Enforcement Administration, No. 1:2015cv00099 (D.R.I. 2015).

[116] American Civil Liberties Union, Press Release, *ACLU Sues Drug Enforcement Agency for Public Records Local Journalist Requested 3 Years Ago* (Mar. 18, 2015), *available at* https://www.aclu.org/news/aclu-sues-drug-enforcement-agency-public-records-local-journalist-requested-3-years-ago.

[117] Letter from David McCraw, Vice President & Assistant Gen. Counsel, The New York Times Company, to Hon. Jason Chaffetz, Chairman, H. Comm. on Oversight & Gov't Reform (May 19, 2015) [hereinafter Letter from The New York Times Company].

[118] *Id.*

[119] Letter from U.S. Postal Serv., to The New York Times Company (Mar. 31, 2014).

[120] Letter from The New York Times Company, *supra* note 115.

[121] Letter from U.S. Postal Inspection Serv., to The New York Times Company (Mar. 2, 2015).

[122] Letter from The New York Times Company, to U.S. Postal Serv. (Mar. 3, 2015); Letter from U.S. Postal Serv., to The New York Times Company (Apr. 28, 2015).

requesters must continue to deal with the original agency, which has little or no say over the timing once the referral is made."[123]

Recently, the Society for Historians of American Foreign Relations (SHAFR) offered recommendations to improve the intra-agency consultation process in its FOIA Implementation Report.[124] SHAFR explains that agency equities are a major factor contributing to FOIA delays. To reduce such delays, SHAFR recommends setting time limits for agencies to act. Also, SHAFR explains that establishing "explicit and specific rules about what can be 'equity' information, strictures as to how long a third party agency can hang onto its interests, and guidelines as to whether particular agency interests can impede the general move to declassification" would fix the equity issue.[125]

Agencies Erect Roadblocks Designed to Close Cases

Federal agencies engage in several practices that create the appearance that they are not interested in actually complying with the requests submitted to them. Instead, agencies create numerous barriers that requesters must overcome before they can receive the requested records. These tactics strain the relationship with requesters and waste resources that should be used to respond to the underlying request.

Unreasonable Standards for a "Reasonable Description"

The FOIA statute requires that requesters provide a reasonable description of the records requested.[126] Requests should be specific enough to permit a professional agency employee familiar with the subject matter to locate the record with a reasonable amount of effort.[127] An agency should carefully consider the nature of each request and give a reasonable interpretation to its content. According to the legislative history, an agency "must be careful not to read [a] request so strictly that the requester is denied information the agency well knows exits in its files, albeit in a different form from that anticipated by the requester."[128]

You need the contract to get the contract

The State FOIA guide asks requesters to provide as much information as the requester has, "such as contract or solicitation number, name of the company awarded the contract,

---

[123] Letter from The New York Times Company, *supra* note 62.
[124] Lauren Harper, *SHAFR Report Calls for Proactive Disclosures, Fixing FOIA Exemption B5, and More.*, UNREDACTED, Jan. 21, 2015, https://nsarchive.wordpress.com/2015/01/21/shafr-report-calls-for-proactive-disclosures-fixing-foia-exemption-b5-and-more/.
[125] *Id.*
[126] 5 U.S.C. § 552.
[127] U.S. Dept. of Justice, *Guide to Freedom of Information Act: Procedural Requirements, available at* http://www.justice.gov/sites/default/files/oip/legacy/2014/07/23/procedural-requirements.pdf (last accessed Sept. 24, 2015).
[128] H.R. REP. NO. 93-876 at 6(1974).

approximate date of the contract, etc."[129] Effectively, State requires a contract number for requests for contracts.

In one instance, a request was submitted for "Copies of contracts with [contractor], commonly known as [contractor], and any final reports generated and delivered by [contractor] to the Department of State over the past 5 years."[130] State rejected the request because "FOIA does not require agencies to do research, to analyze data, to answer written questions, or to create records in response to a request. Answering your request would involve researching all Department files for the documents requested, identifying the times and locations of performance and creating a list, i.e., a record of those documents."[131] Instead, State pointed the requesters to USASpending, which has notoriously inaccurate data.[132] State's refusal to search its database of contracts by the name of the contractor demonstrates a willful disregard for the law, particularly when a keyword search is how they would likely conduct any other search of records.

Too big is not the same as too vague

A request is unreasonably broad if a reasonable agency employee familiar with the subject matter would not be able to identify the records or it would be overly burdensome to search for the records. The number of responsive records alone does not make the request unduly burdensome. The determinative factor is whether the agency can identify with specificity what records the requester is seeking. The volume of responsive records is not part of that determination.[133]

In January 2013, the Taxpayer Protection Alliance (TPA) submitted a request to the General Services Administration (GSA) for all emails mentioning the U.S. Green Building Council or "USGBC."[134] The GSA FOIA office conducted the search and found 70,000 documents.[135] At that point, GSA contacted TPA and asked that they "please revise your request by providing us with specifics such as email traffic between a specific person to another, or some greater detail. As is we had more than 70,000 hits."[136] In response, TPA reiterated their request for all of the materials. GSA, however, continued to push TPA to narrow the scope of the request. [137]

---

[129] U.S. Dep't of State, *Information Access Guide*, *available at* http://foia.state.gov/Request/Guide.aspx (last visited May 31, 2015).

[130] MuckRock, *Copies of contracts between the State Dep't & SecDev*, https://www.muckrock.com/foi/united-states-of-america-10/copies-of-contracts-between-the-state-department-and-secdev-11395/ (last visited May 31, 2015).

[131] *Id.*

[132] *Id.; See* Gov't Accountability Office, *DATA Transparency: Oversight Needed to Address Underreporting & Inconsistencies on Fed. Award Website* (June 2014) (GAO-14-476).

[133] *See, e.g.,* Yeager v. DEA, 678 F.2d 315, 322, 326 (D.C. Cir. 1982) (holding request encompassing over one million computerized records to be valid because "[t]he linchpin inquiry is whether the agency is able to determine 'precisely what records [are] being requested'" (quoting legislative history)).

[134] Letter from Taxpayers Prot. Alliance to Gen. Serv. Admin. (Jan. 17, 2013).

[135] Email from Gen. Serv. Admin. to Taxpayers Prot. Alliance (Nov. 7, 2013, 8:39 a.m.) [hereinafter Nov. 7, 2013, GSA Email].

[136] *Id.*

[137] *See* e.g., Email from Gen. Serv. Admin. to Taxpayers Prot. Alliance (June 18, 2013, 10:04 a.m).; email from Taxpayers Prot. Alliance to Gen. Serv. Admin. (June 26, 2013, 1:16 p.m.).

GSA claimed that TPA did not reasonably describe the documents and attempted to close the request.[138] TPA responded with a clear articulation of the documents it was seeking:[139]

On Mon, Aug 12, 2013 at 3:37 PM, David Williams ▮▮▮▮▮▮▮▮▮▮▮▮▮▮▮▮▮▮▮ wrote:
Ms. Slappy,

Our request was reasonably described. "Reasonably described" is the statutory requirement that goes to making a FOIA request in a manner such that records can be located using reasonable efforts. Emails are easily searchable by key words/key terms, and GSA has apparently done so here. "Reasonably described" does not speak to the size of the response to a FOIA request; it speaks to the burden on the agency to identify and locate the records requested – the request must "be sufficient . . . to enable a professional employee of the agency who was familiar with the subject area of the request to locate the record with a reasonable amount of effort." H.R. Rept. No. 93-876, 93d Cong. 2d Sess. (1974) at 6. The Department of Justice points out that the amount of effort may be very extensive and burdensome without being "unreasonable." DOJ, FOIA Counselor, Vol. I, No. 2 (1980); see also Freedom Watch, Inc. v. CIA, No. 12-0721, 2012 WL

4753281 (D.D.C. Oct. 5, 2012) ("reasonably described" goes to whether FOIA requests are "so broad as to impose an unreasonable burden upon the agency.").

We are therefore legally entitled to the records identified (subject to any exemptions) at appropriate cost. GSA has already identified and located the responsive documents – "hits" – through a minimally burdensome electronic records search using targeted search terms (key words). GSA is at this point declining to produce documents that it has already identified and located, for no legally excusable reason. We therefore repeat our request for the prompt delivery of the responsive documents, and ask GSA to provide a cost estimate for their production. We will of course accept the documents electronically (e.g., by compact disc or file) to further reduce any de minimis burden on GSA. We trust that you are not "closing the file" as you suggested GSA might do, or denying our FOIA request, but will attend to our request promptly and in accordance with the law.

TPA was able to keep the request open and eventually asked for a cost estimate. GSA provided the information necessary to calculate the fees but failed to provide a clear estimate, because "We don't want to charge you for information that is not responsive to your request."[140] Finally, eight months after initially attempting to close the case and TPA's repeated requests that the case be kept open, GSA did close the case.[141] Despite repeated attempts to assure GSA that TPA did, in fact, want all of the documents, GSA continued to assert that some of the documents might not be of interest:[142]

---

[138] Email from Gen. Serv. Admin. to Taxpayers Prot. Alliance (Aug. 11, 2013, 6:36 p.m.).
[139] Email from Taxpayers Prot. Alliance to Gen. Serv. Admin. (Aug. 12, 2013, 3:37 p.m.).
[140] Nov. 7, 2013, GSA Email, *supra* note 79.
[141] Email from Gen. Serv. Admin. to Taxpayers Prot. Alliance (Mar. 10, 2014, 2:48 p.m.).
[142] *Id.*

> Good Afternoon:
>
> In checking back with our business line, there were 70,000 hits with the information provided to pull. There is no confirmation that any of these hits is related to your area of interest.
>
> We did not submit a fee estimate to you because there was no way of telling if any of this information is responsive to your request, therefore no fees were requested or collected.
>
> We asked that you resubmit your request with greater detail, because the request was too vague.
>
> I closed this request on August 11, 2013, I believe on August 12, 2013, you asked that it be reopened: in doing so you expressed why you believed it to be clear and reasonably described. Nothing has changed since that date, our business line still considers the subject offered to vague. This matter is closed.

The truly troubling part of this story is the failure of the Executive Branch to make a good faith effort to respond to the request. At no point in the correspondence does GSA provide an explanation of how they know that the 70,000 documents are not responsive to the request. GSA does not know because after conducting the search and finding numerous documents GSA determined that TPA could not possibly want what TPA repeatedly said it wanted. GSA is not hearing TPA because GSA seems to think that they know more about what TPA wants than TPA. Given that TPA confirmed their interest and willingness to pay associated fees, GSA was obligated to provide responsive records.

The Waiting Game

Hurry up and Wait

Sharyl Attkisson, an investigative journalist, submitted a FOIA request to the Center for Disease Control (CDC) in early December 2014.[143] On December 24, 2014, she received a letter demanding that her request be narrowed or else her case would be closed:[144]

---

[143] Email from Sharyl Attkisson to Centers for Disease Control (Dec. 14, 2014, 9:41 p.m.).
[144] Letter from Centers for Disease Control to Sharyl Attkisson (Dec. 24, 2014).

Dear Ms. Attkisson:

This letter is in response to your Centers for Disease Control and Prevention and Agency for Toxic Substances and Disease Registry (CDC/ATSDR) Freedom of Information Act (FOIA) request of December 14, 2014, pertaining to all materials, emails and/or other records that refer to acute flaccid myelitis and/or unexplained paralysis in children including, but not limited to, reports and/or information from states.

Your request, as written, is extremely broad and covers a large time frame. To fully process your request would require a lengthy search by CDC staff for an unlimited number of records and would be extremely costly for you. The search would involve thousands of pages that would have to be manually searched and numerous electronic files that would have to be searched and reviewed before release for material that is exempt under the Act. In order to search and review records for the request as written, it would take the Agency many months to complete its response. Because we must conserve scarce government resources and because of the scope of your request, we must ask you to narrow its scope and possibly its timeframe.

Additionally, once the scope of your request has been narrowed, it would be processed by the court-approved practice of handling backlogged FOIA requests on a "first-in, first-out" basis. After the lengthy search, the actual processing time for your request would depend on where it falls in the queue and upon the complexity of those ahead of yours.

If you wish to pursue a narrowed request, please send us a new letter reflecting the new scope of your request. **If we do not receive a response from you within 15 days, we will consider this request withdrawn.**

Ms. Attkisson responded within 30 minutes of receiving the above letter and narrowed the request accordingly.[145] She also requested confirmation that her request was not closed. Hearing nothing from the CDC for the remainder of the day on Christmas Eve, Ms. Attkisson emailed again on the next business day, December 26.[146] Still receiving no response, she emailed again on December 29.[147] Finally, Ms. Attkisson received confirmation that her request was successfully narrowed to two custodians over a period of less than six months for documents and emails about a specific issue.[148]

More than two months later the CDC sent a letter stating, "[a] search is currently being conducted by program staff for the documents you requested. . . .We are unable to give you an exact timeframe for completion of your request. Please be assured, however, that a response will be sent to you as quickly as possible."[149] Agencies are required to provide an estimate, but "as quickly as possible" is not an actual estimate.

You aren't still interested are you?

---

[145] Email from Sharyl Attkisson to Centers for Disease Control (Dec. 24, 2014, 10:48 a.m.).
[146] Email from Sharyl Attkisson to Centers for Disease Control (Dec. 26, 2014, 3:39 p.m.).
[147] Email from Sharyl Attkisson to Centers for Disease Control (Dec. 29, 2014, 11:26 a.m.).
[148] Letter from Centers for Disease Control to Sharyl Attkisson (Mar. 4, 2015).
[149] Letter from Centers for Disease Control to Sharyl Attkisson (Mar. 4, 2015).

The "still interested" letter, such as the one received by Ms. Attkisson included above, is a common tactic of agencies to close requests. Simply, agencies demand requesters respond within a specific, limited period of time to simply confirm they are still interested in receiving the requested records.[150] These letters are often sent well after the agency has failed to comply with the statutory deadline for responding to the request. Perhaps even more problematic, some agencies send multiple "still interested" letters prior to even starting to process the request. Complaints about the practice prompted DOJ OIP to issue guidance clarifying basic courtesies such as, "agencies should, at a minimum, have already provided the requester with an acknowledgment of his or her request," and "absent good cause, an agency should not inquire more than once."[151]

The Committee received information about two cases from the Project on Government Oversight (POGO) that show agencies are spending resources on trying to close cases without producing documents, rather than actually trying to respond to the request. In the first case, POGO explained that the DOJ called in 2014 to confirm whether POGO was "still interested in the records" from a request submitted nearly three years earlier.[152]

In another case, POGO received an inquiry in 2014 about a FOIA request originally submitted in 2011.[153] POGO responded:[154]

---------- Forwarded message ----------
From: **Scott Amey** ██████████████
Date: Fri, Dec 5, 2014 at 3:24 PM
Subject: FOIA 11-F-1191
To: ██████████████ @mail.mil

We are still very interested in receiving the requested information. This request has been open so long that Ms. Smithberger, the original requester in 2011, has left POGO, graduated from a master program, worked for years on the Hill, and will return to POGO in a few weeks.

Please process the request.

Scott H. Amey
General Counsel

Agencies Use Fees as a Barrier to Public Access

Fees can be a confusing and frustrating part of the FOIA process. The statute lays out a fee structure based on the category of requester and the intended use of the records. Fees are

---

[150] OGIS, "Play Under Review: Agency Use of "Still Interested" Letters" (Aug. 28, 2015), ,*available at* http://foia.blogs.archives.gov/2015/08/28/play-under-review-agency-use-of-still-interested-letters/ (last accessed Sept. 24, 2015)

[151] Dep't of Justice, *Limitations on Use of "Still-Interested" Inquiries* (July 20, 2015), *available at* http://www.justice.gov/oip/oip-guidance-8 (last accessed Sept. 24, 2015).

[152] Email from Dep't of Justice to Project on Gov't Oversight (May 13, 2014, 3:24 p.m.).

[153] Email from Project on Gov't Oversight to Dep't of Justice (Dec. 5, 2014, 3:24 p.m.).

[154] *Id.*

permissible to the extent that they cover the cost of the work being done; however, fees collected are not returned to the agency that charged them. Instead, all fees collected are deposited in the general fund of the United States Treasury. This process allows the Federal government to recoup some of the cost of some requests, without encouraging agencies to turn FOIA responses into a revenue generation stream. Unfortunately, excessive and poorly articulated fee estimates give the public reason to suspect that the agency is using the fees to deter requesters. Stubborn refusals for fee waivers in the public interest and refusals to recognize news media further contribute to that impression.

Exorbitant Fee Estimates Make FOIA Unusable

One of the most outrageous fee estimates came from a March 2014 FOIA request sent to the Drug Enforcement Agency (DEA) asking for records related to the capture of Mexican drug lord Joaquin "El Chapo" Guzman.[155] According to MuckRock, an organization that assists the public in submitting FOIA requests, the requester in this case received what is likely the largest ever fee estimate for a FOIA request.[156] After receiving an acknowledgement from the DEA approximately two weeks after the initial request was received, the requester and the DEA corresponded about the status of the request. The requester finally received a response letter nearly a year later in January 2015 identifying 13,051 case files potentially responsive to the request. According to the letter, the estimated search fee for the request was $1,461,712. MuckRock provided the following analysis of the fee estimate:

> In fairness, the request is quite broad in scope, and the estimated 13,051 case files would create considerable workload. But assuming that $200,000 of that fee came from photocopying (which would put the total number pages at two million), that would put the time estimate at over 40,000 hours, or 1785 days. That's almost five years of constant work without breaks. The DEA might want to look into a more efficient system for processing—or invest in a redaction drone.[157]

Large fees often are prohibitive, and many private individuals cannot afford to pay them. An example submitted to the Committee involved a request submitted to the National Oceanic and Atmospheric Administration (NOAA) in April 2015.[158] The request asked for 11 specific records. Within about three weeks, NOAA responded with an exorbitant fee estimate for processing the request.[159] NOAA claimed it would cost the agency $45,310.86 to search for the records, $19,732.97 to review the records, and $435.20 to duplicate the records.[160] Two weeks later, NOAA sent another letter with an updated fee estimate of $45,579.02.[161] The revised

---

[155] Dave Maass, *Happy Sunshine Week: Introducing The Foilies, Round 1*, ELECTRONIC FRONTIER FOUNDATION, Mar. 16, 2015, https://www.eff.org/deeplinks/2015/03/happy-sunshine-week-introducing-foilies.
[156] JPat Brown, *DEA wants $1.4 million before it will begin processing request*, MUCKROCK, Feb. 5, 2015, https://www.muckrock.com/news/archives/2015/feb/05/dea-wants-14-million-it-will-begin-processing-requ/.
[157] *Id.*
[158] Letter from Shankman Leone, P.A., to Nat'l Oceanic & Atmospheric Admin. Office of Gen. Counsel (Apr. 22, 2015).
[159] Letter from Nat'l Oceanic & Atmospheric Admin. to Shankman Leone, P.A. (May 15, 2015).
[160] *Id.*
[161] Letter from Nat'l Oceanic & Atmospheric Admin. to Shankman Leone, P.A. (May 28, 2015).

estimate did not include any fees for review. It also slightly reduced both the estimated search and duplication fees.

In the most recent fee estimate, NOAA approximated the cost for duplication at $427.20.[162] Under 15 C.F.R. 4.11, National Marine Fisheries Service charges $0.16 per page for paper or the direct cost plus operator time for other reproduction, which presumably would be very quick to copy onto a disk. This would mean that for a $427.20 estimated duplication fee, NOAA anticipates duplication of 2,670 pages.

The same CFR section provides that the agency may charge the salary rate of the employee plus 16 percent for manual search or actual direct cost, plus the cost of operator time for a computerized search. NOAA estimates the search fees at $45,151.82.[163] Assuming a relatively high rate of $75 per hour, NOAA would expend 602 hours on search time alone to identify just 2,671 pages. This is excessive for a relatively small number of estimated documents. If this request did, in fact, require 602 hours of search time, the agency should include an explanation in the letter. Instead, the requester received a letter providing the estimated cost with no explanation for this exorbitant estimate.

Smaller Fees Can Also Be Problematic

Agencies often quibble over small amounts, denying requests for waivers, or insisting that a release is not in the public interest. In March 2015, the FOIA Resource Center submitted a FOIA request to U.S. Customs and Border Patrol (CBP) and included a request for a fee waiver, stating that the requested documents were "in the public interest."[164] About two weeks later, CBP responded by denying the request for a fee waiver and estimating processing fees of $60.50.[165]

The requester appealed the fee waiver denial and fee estimate. Despite the relatively low estimate of $60.50, CBP composed a lengthy legal memo explaining how they determined the request not to be "in the public interest."[166] The memo laid out detailed requirements necessary to prove to CBP that the request would be in the public interest.[167] However, agencies are not supposed to charge fees if the cost of collecting the fee would exceed the amount a requester would be charged. The drafting of such a memo presumably cost more than the $60.50 fee charged.[168]

Another example of questionable fee practices submitted to the Committee showed that the agency categorized fees beyond the standard FOIA breakdown: search, review, and duplication. A requester submitted a FOIA request to the Air Force and, when asked, the

---

[162] *Id.*

[163] *Id.*

[164] *See* Letter from U.S. Customs & Border Protection to FOIA Resource Center (May 4, 2015).

[165] *Id.*

[166] *Id.*

[167] *Id.*

[168] *Id.*

requestor even provided the FOIA officer with the exact location of the document.[169] Nonetheless, the Air Force responded with a fee estimate of $220.00, which was further broken down into unusual categories.[170] The reviewer claimed "search: 2.0 hours," "computer search: 2.0 hours," and "review: 3.0 hours."[171] It is unclear what the difference is between search and computer search, but it seems unreasonable to search for four hours when the requester identified the exact database.

The Committee also heard from a freelance journalist who filed two separate FOIA requests to the Office of Foreign Assets Control (OFAC) in January 2015.[172] In both instances, OFAC denied the requester a fee waiver. The request indicated that the responsive records were in the public interest and provided OFAC with evidence that he had more than five years of professional experience and stated that he had recently and consistently published articles in well-known news outlets and, therefore, had a reasonable expectation of publication. Under these circumstances, OFAC was obligated to treat the requester as a member of the media, and waive the fee.[173] The requester believes that OFAC denied his fee waiver requests because he did not have a publication contract, even though the FOIA statute does not require such a contract.

Two requests to the IRS from the Committee for Efficient Government (CFEG) provide another example of either incompetence or deliberate malfeasance. CFEG submitted FOIA requests to the Internal Revenue Service (IRS)—one in August 2012 and the other in August 2013.[174] The IRS denied fee waivers for both requests on the basis that the requester was "commercial."[175] According to CFEG's website, "CFEG's mission is to seek and explore ways in which the Government can operate more efficiently and bring those ideas and solutions to the forefront of Congress and the American public"[176]—hardly a commercial interest. Upon appeal, the agency refused to engage in the legally required level of review and continues to claim that CFEG's request is a commercial interest, without any explanation.[177]

The Biggest Barrier of All: Delay, Delay, Delay

Each agency is required to determine within 20 working days after the receipt of a FOIA request whether the records will be released or the agency intends to withhold all or some of the requested records, pursuant to FOIA's exemptions. The 20 day response period begins on the

---

[169] Email from U.S. Air Force to Joseph Page (Apr. 24, 2015, 9:37 a.m.); email from Joseph Page to U.S. Air Force (Apr. 24, 2015 10:47 a.m.).
[170] Email from U.S. Air Force to Joseph Page (May 13, 2015, 5:09 p.m.).
[171] *Id.*
[172] Email from Daniel DeFraia to H. Comm. on Oversight & Gov't Reform (May 9, 2015, 11:40 a.m.).
[173] 5 U.S.C. § 552(a)(4)(ii)-(iii).
[174] *See* Letter from Scott Hodes to Internal Revenue Serv. (Nov. 18, 2013).
[175] Letter from Internal Revenue Serv. to Kenneth Hemmerle, II (Apr. 2, 2013); Letter from Internal Revenue Serv. to Scott Hodes (Sept. 11, 2013).
[176] Comm. for Efficient Gov't, *Mission Statement, available at* http://cfegov.wpengine.com/mission-statement/ (last accessed May 29, 2015).
[177] Letter from Scott Hodes to Hon. Jason Chaffetz, Chairman, H. Comm. on Oversight & Gov't Reform (May 18, 2015).

date the request is first received by the appropriate component of the agency, but no later than ten days after any component of the agency receives the request. Processing a request is not the same as providing requested records. The actual disclosure of records is required to follow promptly after the processing of a request.

While FOIA requests are meant to be processed in a timely manner, the law provides extensions to accommodate certain situations. Agencies can extend the timeline to process a request by up to 10 days if the agency can claim an "unusual circumstance"—defined as the need to collect records from remote locations, review larger numbers of records, or consult with other agencies.[178] Agencies must inform the requester of the delay, provide the date the determination is expected, and give the requester the opportunity to limit the scope of the request and/or arrange with the agency a negotiated deadline for processing the request.

While the Committee fully understands the need for extensions for "unusual circumstances," some agencies willfully underfund their FOIA offices or violate laws that govern FOIA processing with little to no explanation. Recent stories of agencies that delay FOIA processing well beyond acceptable timelines with no legitimate reasons have caused an erosion of trust between the Executive Branch and the American public. The Committee has received numerous examples of FOIA abuses that illustrate this problem.

A FOIA response case study

Syracuse University conducted a study of agency responses to FOIA requests. Syracuse filed identical requests at 21 agencies for "a case-by-case listing of all FOIA requests received by the FOIA office from October 1, 2012 – December 31, 2014" with certain specific data fields.[179] This should be a simple request because all of the records are in the FOIA office and the database should be frequently accessed.

After four months, only seven agencies provided records.[180] While four of the remaining 14 agencies appeared to be making an effort to respond, ten agencies showed delinquent efforts to comply with the law. Three agencies failed to respond at all.[181] Three acknowledged the request but failed to provide any additional information or additional correspondence. Three agencies "provided records that were clearly unresponsive." The last agency, the CIA, denied the request because it required an "unreasonable effort."[182]

Syracuse highlighted responses from two agencies. First, "[The Department of Homeland Security Immigration and Customs Enforcement's (ICE)] response has been typical of our dealings with them. At first the agency sent a broken CD. Then they sent a new CD with

---

[178] 5 U.S.C. § 552(a)(6)(B).

[179] *See, e.g.,* Letter from Transactional Records Access Clearinghouse, Syracuse University, to Info. & Privacy Coordinator, Central Intelligence Agency, (Jan. 23, 2014).

[180] Letter from Transactional Records Access Clearinghouse, Syracuse University, to H. Comm. on Oversight & Gov't Reform (May 19, 2015).

[181] *Id.*

[182] *Id.*

only one month out of the 27 months of data. Then they became unresponsive, forcing us to appeal."[183]

Similarly, the Department of Justice's Office of Information Policy, the federal agency that provides guidance to other agencies on FOIA processes, acknowledged receipt after 20 working days and failed to follow up with any additional information after the initial acknowledgement.

State delays research

On July 26, 2013, a Ph.D. candidate at the University of Virginia made a FOIA request to the State Department.[184] The expected completion date was July 2014. The State Department subsequently extended the completion date three times without an explanation.[185] The new completion date is now April 2016, leaving the requester with a total waiting time of two years and nine months.[186]

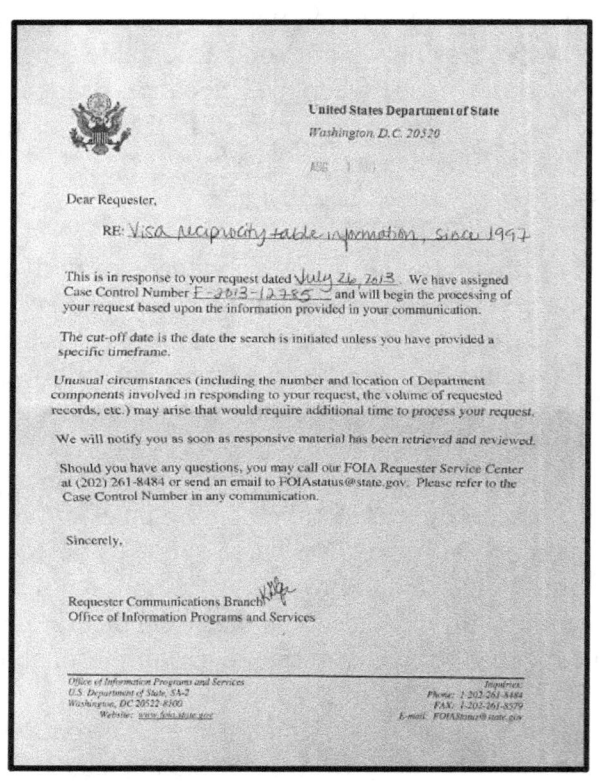

While the request was submitted via an online portal, State responded with a paper form completed by hand and sent through the mail. The signature line is left blank but there appears to be a set of initials next to the title.[187] The outdated processes exemplified by this practice are almost certainly a symptom of larger inefficiencies and ineffective policies that contribute to the extensive delays at State.

State has also kept the Huffington Post's Ryan Reilly in a similar limbo on a FOIA request he made in May 2013. Reilly requested a copy of the memorandum that Secretary Clinton reportedly sent President Obama regarding Guantanamo Bay. Mr. Reilly received an estimated completion date of September 2014, but has yet to receive a response.[188]

Delays cost the taxpayer

The public should not need to file a lawsuit in order to get the information that they are already entitled to by law. Delays waste time and taxpayer money. One particularly egregious

---

[183] *Id.*

[184] *See* Email from U.S. Dep't of State, FOIA to Steven Liao (July 26, 2013, 1:30 p.m.).

[185] *See* Email from Steven Liao to H. Comm. on Oversight & Gov't Reform (May 14, 2015, 12:09 a.m.).

[186] *See* Email from Steven Liao to H. Comm. on Oversight & Gov't Reform (November 12, 2015, 2:52 p.m.).

[187] Letter from Requester Communications Branch, Office of Information Programs & Services, U.S. Dep't of State, to Steven Liao, Requester, (Aug. 1, 2013).

[188] Email from Ryan Reilly to H. Comm. on Oversight & Gov't Reform (May 5, 2015, 1:58 p.m.).

example of this involves a May 15, 2014, FOIA request by the *New York Times* to EOUSA for documents related to attorney's fees during a six year period.[189] EOUSA was unresponsive. Despite more than 10 attempts to contact the EOUSA for an update, EOUSA did not respond. The *New York Times* eventually filed suit in November 2014, which led to the United States Attorney's Office providing the documents and EOUSA paying for the *New York Times*' legal fees.[190]

Requesters shouldn't need a lawsuit to get responsive documents

A FOIA request for documents relating to the requester's own communications and travel was sent to Customs and Border Protection (CBP) on July 23, 2014. Having received no response within 20 working days, the requester sent two additional letters to CBP. Again, the requestor received no response. Thinking something must be wrong with the original request, the requester submitted the same request again, only for the agency to close it as "duplicative."[191]

In March 2015, in another attempt to get a response, the requester filed an appeal, claiming constructive denial. The agency closed the appeal, however, finding "no adverse decision for the Appeals Office to review."[192] The only other option for the requester was a lawsuit. Instead of incurring these costs, the requester informed the Committee he would continue to wait. On May 8 2015, the CBP FOIA website showed the request was "in the 'Assignment' phase, to be completed in September of [2014.]"[193]

On May 20, 2015, the Committee requested information from multiple agencies about several FOIA requests about which we had received complaints including the above mentioned request.[194] On May 27, seven days after the Committee's letter and more than ten months since the request was submitted, the requester received a final response.[195] In total, the requester received 22 pages and the agency did not claim any pages were withheld under exemptions.[196]

A year's worth of data takes more time than that to process

Bill Alpert of *Barrons* reported to the Committee that on February 5, 2013, he submitted a FOIA request to the Social Security Administration (SSA) for documents that show how the agency's actuaries calculate forecasts.[197] While SSA provided some information, it did not

---

[189] Letter from The New York Times Company, *supra* note 62.
[190] *See* New York Times v. United States Department of Justice, *No.* t4-cv-9 149 (S.D.N.Y. Nov. 18, 2014).
[191] Email from Owen Barcala to H. Comm. on Oversight & Gov't Reform (May 8, 2015, 5:28 p.m.).
[192] *Id.*
[193] *Id.*
[194] Letter from Hon. Jason Chaffetz, Chairman, H. Comm. on Oversight & Gov't Reform to Hon. Jeh C. Johnson, Sec. U.S. Dept. Homeland Security (May 20, 2015), Letter from Hon. Jason Chaffetz, Chairman, H. Comm. on Oversight & Gov't Reform to Hon. Loretta E. Lynch, Attorney General U.S. Dept. Justice (May 20, 2015), Letter from Hon. Jason Chaffetz, Chairman, H. Comm. on Oversight & Gov't Reform to Hon. John F. Kerry, Sec. U.S. Dept. State (May 20, 2015), Letter from Hon. Jason Chaffetz, Chairman, H. Comm. on Oversight & Gov't Reform to Hon. John Koskinen, Comm'r. U.S. Dept. Treasury, Internal Revenue Service (May 20, 2015).
[195] Email from Owen Barcala to H. Comm. on Oversight & Gov't Reform (June 1, 2015, 1:43 p.m).
[196] *Id.*
[197] Email from William Alpert to H. Comm. on Oversight & Gov't Reform (May 11, 2015) [hereinafter May 11, 2015, Email to H. Comm.].

provide the complete information necessary to replicate the predictions. More than one year ago, SSA promised Mr. Alpert "one-year's worth of programs and spreadsheets," which he still has yet to receive.[198] After he contacted the Chief Actuary at SSA to set up an interview in preparation for his article, *Social Security's Predictions: Off by a $1 Trillion*, he began to receive messages from the SSA FOIA office explaining how the office wanted to help him but that it would take a month to gather the documents, and the office could not afford to take the time to do so.[199]

While long delays in responding to FOIA requests are a problem, the issue becomes compounded when poor agency practices lead to longer delays. As Mr. Alpert puts it, "[t]his should have been an easy, uncontroversial FOIA request, if the Social Security actuaries were doing their work in a way that kept pace with most data analysts."[200] If Mr. Alpert's assertion is correct, that SSA is not keeping pace with the methods of current data analysts, then these delays become even more unacceptable since it would mean that the agency cannot follow the law because of, at least in part, agency incompetence.

Unreasonable Delay in Determining an Unreasonable Description

Let Freedom Ring submitted a FOIA request to the Department of Treasury on May 13, 2013.[201] The Department of Treasury immediately notified Mr. Hanna, with Let Freedom Ring, that his request was being forwarded to the Internal Revenue Service, which would correspond directly with him.[202] Mr. Hanna was subsequently contacted by the IRS on four different occasions between June 2013 and October 2013, explaining that the IRS needed more time to complete the request.[203] Five months after his original request, Mr. Hanna had still not been informed about which documents, if any, the IRS would produce. Finally, on April 9, 2015, two years after the initial request, the IRS told Mr. Hanna that it would be unable to complete his FOIA request because the request does not reasonably describe the documents.[204]

A two year period for a completion date is unreasonable, but two years to even read the request is outrageous. There is no reason the IRS could not have made this determination within the statutory deadline. Delays like this diminish the American public's confidence that its government is working to serve the public good.

"Something is desperately wrong with this process"

A requester from Florida sums up the issue of delays in FOIA succinctly when she explained that "[s]omething is desperately wrong with this process. It is either totally broken or requests are intentionally being ignored."[205] These frustrations stem from her experience with a FOIA request from May 16, 2014 to FEMA. The request covered information about an agency

---

[198] Letter from Social Security Admin. to William Alpert, (Mar. 19, 2014).
[199] May 11, 2015 Email to H. Comm., *supra* note 128.
[200] May 11, 2015 Email to H. Comm., *supra* note 128.
[201] Letter from Colin A. Hanna to U.S. Dep't of the Treasury (May 13, 2013).
[202] Letter from U.S. Dep't of the Treasury to Colin A. Hanna (May 14, 2013).
[203] *See, e.g.,* Letter from Internal Rev. Serv. to Colin A. Hanna (Oct. 18, 2013).
[204] Letter from Internal Rev. Serv. to Colin A. Hanna (Apr. 9, 2015).
[205] Email from Ms. Calvert to H. Comm. on Oversight & Gov't Reform (May 10, 2015, 7:59 a.m.).

grant. Despite making multiple attempts for an update and bringing the issue to a supervisor, she "received nothing but delays."[206]

It is unreasonable to expect citizens to maintain trust in a government that simply ignores them when they make requests for information. The consequences of these extreme delays could have serious and far reaching effects. People expect their government to be responsive, not to stonewall them when a response is inconvenient.

Conclusion

The FOIA process is broken. Hundreds of thousands of requests are made each year and hundreds of thousands of requests are backlogged, marked with inappropriate redactions, or otherwise denied. More experienced requesters push through the process in hopes of eventually receiving something. Less experienced requesters are shocked at the delays and procedural burdens. In the end, agencies close more than 40 percent of requests without releasing even one document.

As David McCraw from the New York Times said, some agencies are good and effective in responding to FOIA requests, while others are consistently unresponsive and show little sign of improvement. Importantly, the obscured view from the outside looking into an agency prohibits requesters and even Congress from developing a nuanced view of exactly each and every hang-up in the process at any agency. What is clear, however, is that those unresponsive agencies lack effective incentives to make improvements.

Whatever the reasons, FOIA has, in many respects, been unacceptably neutered. As this report outlines, obfuscation comes in many forms: impermissible delays, exorbitant fees, improper use of exemptions, and denial by never-ending referrals are just a few. Nothing makes government more accountable than making its actions open and transparent to those who are paying the bills. Structural reform is necessary to ensure the FOIA tool works as intended. Legislation is needed to clarify existing requirements and impose additional requirements that will ensure agencies to comply with legal obligations to make government public.

---

[206] *Id.*

Appendix

FCC Documents